Mastering

MacBook Air 2024

The Comprehensive Step-by-Step Guide to Mastering
Apple's Most Advanced and Elegant M3-Powered Laptop
with Tips & Tricks for Beginners and Seniors

Lyra Harper

TABLE OF CONTENTS

INTRODUCTION

Apple Inc. produces a range of Mac computers known as the MacBook Air. Apple began utilizing their own Apple silicon M-series chips in the Air in 2020, replacing Intel processors. Currently available with 13-inch and 15-inch screens, the MacBook Air is Apple's entry-level laptop in the current product line, falling short of the MacBook Pro in terms of performance. In November 2020, Apple announced the MacBook Air equipped with the Apple M1 system on a chip. The first 15-inch MacBook Air was introduced in June 2023, and a revised edition based on the Apple M2 CPU was released in July 2022. Apple released MacBook Airs with M3 chips in March 2024, available in 13- and 15-inch variants.

M3

A series of ARM-based system-on-a-chips (SoCs) is what is regarded as the Apple M3 and was created by Apple Inc. as a central processing unit (CPU) and graphics processing unit (GPU) for their Mac notebooks and desktop computers. It is a part of the Apple Silicon series. Following the transition from Intel Core to Apple silicon and released in late 2023, it is the third version of ARM architecture designed for Apple's Mac computers, following the Apple M2.

GPU

Hardware-accelerated ray tracing, mesh shading, and dynamic caching are some of the characteristics of the new GPU. In real-time, local memory is allocated using the Dynamic Caching technology. In contrast to traditional methods, Dynamic Caching guarantees that just the amount of memory needed for a job is used, optimizing memory usage and improving performance and efficiency. This is especially helpful for tasks requiring a lot of graphics, where dynamic memory allocation can be crucial.

NPU

The A17 Pro's 35 TOPS NPU, found in the iPhone 15 Pro series, is faster than the M3's 16-core Neural Engine, equipped with specialized neural network hardware, and can perform over 18 trillion operations per second.

AI

Apple's Neural Engine and the M3 Max's higher maximum RAM (128 GiB) were designed with AI development and workloads in mind, enabling AI models with a large number of parameters. When it comes to AI workloads, Apple says the M3 performs 15% better than the M2 (the prior iteration).

Memory

The Unified Memory Architecture (UMA) of the M3 SoCs uses 6,400 MT/s LPDDR5 SDRAM, which is comparable to that of the M2 generation. Similar to previous M series SoCs, these functions as video RAM in addition to RAM. Memory controller counts for the M3, M3 Pro, and M3 Max are 8, 12, and 32 respectively. Each controller can access up to 4 GB of memory and is 16 bits wide. Memory bandwidth is less on the 14-core M3 Max and M3/M2 Pro than it is on the M1/M2 Pro. With a 192-bit memory bus compared to a 256-bit bus for the M1 and M2 Pro, the M3 Pro can process data at a speed of just 150 GB/sec, while its predecessors could process 200 GB/sec. The 16-core M3 Max has the same 400 GB/sec as the previous M1 and M2 Max models, whereas the 14-core M3 Max only activates 24 of the 32 controllers, giving it 300 GB/sec as opposed to 400 GB/sec for all models of the M1 and M2 Max. A PCI Express storage controller, a USB4 controller with Thunderbolt 4 capability, a Secure Enclave, and an image signal processor (ISP) are among the additional parts.

What's New

Widgets on your desktop

For convenient access, add widgets from your preferred apps to your desktop. You may add your iPhone widgets to your Mac without installing the relevant programs by using Continuity.

Video conferencing

To add a layer between your shared screen and your video, use Presenter Overlay. With a simple hand motion, respond to the discussion with 3D effects such as hearts, confetti, or fireworks. You can share one or more apps directly from the window you're in. Take charge of the way your film is put together when you use an iPhone or Studio Display as your camera.

Add sections and columns to your reminder lists

Sort similar reminders into sections according to your preference for column visualization. Additionally, it's simple to make grocery lists that divide products into several parts automatically.

Organize your browsing with web apps and profiles in Safari

Convert your preferred websites into web-based applications so you can quickly access them from the Dock at any time. You can benefit from the safety of increased private browsing and maintain a professional distance from your private life by creating profiles. Look at what more macOS Sonoma is capable of: Create links from one note to a different one; share passkeys and passwords with a select number of trusted contacts; utilize Game Mode to automatically assign games high priority on the CPU and GPU of your Mac; and much more. You can even add a slow-motion screensaver of a landscape, cityscape, or seascape and set it as your wallpaper.

Overview of This Book

Chapter 1: MacBook Air at a Glance

This chapter provides a full overview of what comes with your MacBook Air, including the Magic Keyboard and Trackpad. The chapter also covers important issues like charging the battery, using various peripherals, and connecting to an external display, so you can get the most out of your new gadget from the start.

Chapter 2: Getting Started

This chapter is a complete guide on configuring and optimizing your Mac. It goes over the initial setup procedure, which includes creating your Apple ID and iCloud, interacting with others via various communication options, taking screenshots, and managing data via backup, restoration, and transfer.

Chapter 3: Using MacBook Air M3 with Other Devices

In this chapter, you will get to explore how to distribute and broadcast material across numerous devices using a variety of technologies. It discusses how to share material between devices, stream media to larger screens with AirPlay, and work efficiently with several devices to increase productivity.

Chapter 4: What is in the Desktop?

This chapter provides a complete tutorial on accessing and using your MacBook's essential features. It covers how to use the Menu bar, operate efficiently on the desktop, and search with Spotlight. It also demonstrates how to rapidly change settings, use Siri, handle notifications, launch programs from the Dock, and arrange files in the Finder.

Chapter 5: The Basics

This chapter covers the most important tasks for utilizing your MacBook successfully. It shows you how to connect to the internet, surf the web, preview files, adjust display brightness, change volume settings, and utilize Touch ID for security and convenience.

Chapter 6: Beyond the Basics

This chapter delves into improving your MacBook experience. You will learn how to minimize your screen time, use voice dictation, and communicate effectively via emails, texts, and video conversations. You'll also learn how to edit photos and videos, as well as how to use Live Text to interact with written material within images.

Chapter 7: Files and Folders

In this chapter, you will learn the fundamentals of managing your digital environment on your MacBook. You will learn how to create and edit documents, combine them into professional-looking PDFs, and organize everything using folders and tags. Furthermore, you'll tackle the critical duty of backing up your data and restoring it if necessary, ensuring that your information is always safe and sound.

Chapter 8: Apps

This chapter focuses on the great world of apps accessible for your MacBook. You'll look at the pre-installed programs that come with your Mac, which are ideal for everyday activities, unleash your creativity, and customize your MacBook experience.

Chapter 9: Customize your Mac

In this chapter, you will learn how to alter your system settings, include and also customize widgets, make the best use of screen saver, including email and other accounts, automate tasks with the use of shortcuts, create memoji, and also ensure that text and other items are seen much bigger on the screen.

Chapter 10: Using Apple Devices Together

If you own an iPhone and a Mac, you will like to make use of these two devices simultaneously. In this chapter, you will learn how to make use of continuity across devices, make use of an iPhone as a webcam, make use of an iPhone with a desk view, have your Mac unlocked with the use of your Apple watch, and you will also learn how to make and receive phone calls.

Chapter 11: Apple ID and iCloud

Your Apple devices cannot work without the use of an Apple ID. In this chapter, you will learn about the diverse ways to make use of Apple ID and also the iCloud. You will also learn about the use of the iCloud+, storing files in iCloud drive and you will also learn how to share and collaborate on these files.

Chapter 12: Family and Friends

One lovely advantage the digital world has now is effective collaboration. In this chapter, you will learn about the various ways in which you can make use of the various apps and configurations on your Mac. You will learn about family sharing as well as how you can set it up. You will also learn how to share purchases with your family, watch content together with your family using SharePlay and you will also learn how best to share a photo library.

Chapter 13: Listen, watch, and read

In this chapter, you will learn how to download and listen to podcasts, read and listen to books, read the news, and also follow important trends in the stock market.

Chapter 14: Subscribe to Services

There are diverse subscriptions you can subscribe to to ensure that you enjoy your Mac and by extension all of your Apple devices. In this chapter, you will be introduced to some of these subscriptions including how to subscribe to them.

Chapter 15: Privacy, Security, and Accessibility

In a world filled with so many cyber threats, this chapter will help you perfectly understand the diverse ways in which you can protect your device. In this chapter, you will learn how to guard your privacy, make use of mail privacy protection, control access to your camera, employ the use of sign-in with Apple for apps and websites, keep your data safe, and you will also learn how to create a passkey. Furthermore, you will learn about the various accessibility features you can make use of, which are vision, hearing, mobility, etc.

Chapter 16: Accessories and Hardware

In the very last chapter of this book, here you will learn about the various accessories and hardware you can use to get the most out of your device.

Now let's get started;

CHAPTER 1

MACBOOK AIR M3 AT A GLANCE

The MacBook Air models that are currently being shipped are the focus of this article. You may obtain information and documentation for other models by visiting the Apple Support article that can assist with model identification if you're unsure about which model you have. **Below are some of the features that both the 13-inch and 15-inch MacBook Air M3 models have;**

- **Thunderbolt / USB 4 ports**: You can power your computer, charge accessories (such as an iPad or a rechargeable trackpad or keyboard), and transmit data at Thunderbolt 3 or USB 4 speeds (up to 40 Gbit/s). A Thunderbolt / USB 4 port can also be used to connect a projector or display. You can use an additional external display with the laptop lid closed on an Apple M3 chip MacBook Air.

- **MagSafe 3 port:** To replenish the MacBook Air's battery, insert the USB-C Power Adapter that comes with it. When the battery needs to be charged, the indicator light flashes amber, and when it is fully charged, it illuminates green. With the optional 70W USB-C Power Adapter, you can quickly charge the battery on your MacBook Air—up to 50% in just 30 minutes.

- **3.5mm headphone jack**: To enjoy your preferred music or movies, connect an external speaker system or stereo headphones. Even without an amplifier or a digital-to-analog converter, you can use high-impedance headphones.

- **1080p FaceTime HD camera**: Take photos and videos or make FaceTime video calls. The camera system performs admirably in low light and produces high-quality footage. The camera is on if the green indication light next to it is glowing.

- **Speakers**: The six-speaker sound system on the 15-inch MacBook Air is made up of two sets of force-canceling woofers and two tweeters. The four speakers of the 13-inch MacBook Air's sound system are made up of two woofers and two tweeters. Enjoy a rich audio experience with both thanks to Dolby Atmos support for movies and music in spatial audio.

- **Touch ID (the power button)**: To switch on your MacBook Air, simply lift the lid or press. Moreover, you can lock your Mac by tapping the Touch ID icon. You must enter your password to log in the first time you boot up or restart. Once Touch ID is configured, you can use it for Apple Pay purchases and verify with a touch rather than inputting your password (following your initial login).

- **Microphones**: With the three built-in microphones, you can record sounds or have conversations with pals. With the M3 chip in the MacBook Air, experience improved speech clarity during audio and video chats.

- **Force Touch trackpad:** Use trackpad gestures to operate your MacBook Air. Because every part of the trackpad surface functions as a button, you can click anywhere with ease.

What's included with your MacBook Air

Two accessories that come in the box are required to utilize your MacBook Air: a cable and one of the power adapters indicated below.

- **USB-C to MagSafe 3 Cable:** To charge your MacBook Air, insert the USB-C to MagSafe 3 Cable into one of the MacBook Air's MagSafe 3 ports and the provided power adapter into the other end. A battery status indication on the connector begins to light when you first attach the cable to the MacBook Air; it is green when the battery is completely charged and amber when it is charging.
- 30W USB-C Power Adapter: for the MacBook Air 13-inch. Completely extend the AC plug's electrical prongs after connecting the power adapter, and then insert the adapter into an AC power outlet.
- **35W Dual USB-C Port Compact Power Adapter:** for MacBook Air 13- and 15-inch models. Completely extend the AC plug's electrical prongs after connecting the power adapter, and then insert the adapter into an AC power outlet.
- **70W USB-C Power Adapter or 67W USB-C Power Adapter:** For the 13- and 15-inch MacBook Air, optional. Completely extend the AC plug's electrical prongs after connecting the power adapter, and then insert the adapter into an AC power outlet. You can quickly charge the MacBook Air to 50% capacity with the 70W USB-C Power Adapter in around 30 minutes.

Note that additional accessories and adapters are available for separate purchase. For availability and additional information, check out apple.com, your neighborhood Apple Store, or other resellers. To ensure you select the correct product, go over the paperwork or get in touch with the manufacturer.

Magic Keyboard for MacBook Air

With just a few keystrokes, you can effortlessly enter emoticons, change keyboard languages, lock your MacBook Air, and carry out numerous system tasks with the Magic Keyboard with Touch ID's built-in functionality. After setting up Touch ID, you may utilize your fingerprint to unlock your MacBook Air, swiftly lock your screen, and use Apple Pay to make purchases online and from the App Store, Apple TV app, and Apple Books.

Set up Touch ID: Touch ID setup is available in Touch ID & Password in System Settings, or during setup. **Turn on your MacBook Air: hit any key, lift the lid, or hit Touch ID, the power button.**

- **Use Touch ID**: Once Touch ID is configured, you will need to enter your password to log in each time you turn on or restart the machine. You can simply authenticate by lightly pressing your finger on the Touch ID sensor whenever you are prompted for your password within the same session after your initial login. Additionally, Apple Pay allows you to safely make online purchases using **Touch ID.**
- **Lock your MacBook Air**: To instantly lock your screen, presses **Touch ID.**
- **Turn off your MacBook Air**: Select the **Apple menu > Shut Down** to switch off your MacBook Air. Select the **Apple menu > Sleep** to put your MacBook Air to sleep.

Use function keys: These frequently used system functions can be accessed more quickly with the function keys in the top row:

- **Brightness (F1, F2)**: Tap the brightness icon to either reduce or increase the brightness of the screen.
- **Mission Control (F3)**: To see everything that's operating on your MacBook Air, including all of your open windows and spaces, press the **Mission Control key.**
- **Spotlight Search (F4)**: To use Spotlight to look for an item on your MacBook Air, press the Spotlight key.
- **Dictation / SIRI (F5)**: To begin dictating text anywhere you can type (such as in Messages, Mail, Pages, as well as other apps), press the Microphone key. Holding **down the Microphone key to bring up Siri, and then speak your request right away.**
- **Do Not Disturb (F6)**: To switch off or on Do Not Disturb, press **the designated key.** On the MacBook Air, Do Not Disturb turns off the ability to see or hear notifications. However, you can see them afterward in the Notification Center.
- **Media (F7, F8, and F9)**: To fast-forward a music, movie, or slideshow, press the Fast-forward key. Alternatively, you can use the Play/Pause and Rewind keys.
- **Mute (F10)**: To turn off the sound from the integrated speakers or the 3.5 mm headphone port, press **the Mute key.**
- **Volume (F11, F12)**: The internal speakers, 3.5 mm headphone port, or Bluetooth audio device can all have their sound levels adjusted by pressing the Decrease or Increase volume keys.

Keep in mind that function keys can be used to execute commands in particular applications or to accomplish different tasks. For instance, the F11 key can display the desktop and hide all open windows. Holding down the Function (Fn)/Globe key while pressing a function key will activate the key's other function.

- **Adjust keyboard settings**: Click **the Keyboard in the sidebar after opening System Settings to customize the keyboard and the Function (Fn)/Globe key.** The brightness and illumination of the keyboard can be adjusted, as well as keyboard shortcuts and whether or not the Function (Fn)/Globe key displays the emoji picker/Character Viewer, alters the input source, or initiates dictation.
- **Use emoji and symbols**: To access the emoji picker, tap the Function (Fn)/Globe key (if you have enabled this feature in the Keyboard settings). Browse emoji by categories or by using the search function when the emoji picker is active. You can also insert icons like pictographs.
- **Learn about keyboard shortcuts**: On your MacBook Air, you may rapidly complete specific operations by pressing key combinations, as well as those that you would typically complete using a mouse or trackpad. To copy the chosen text, for instance,

press **Command-C**. Then, click the location where you intend to paste the text and hit **Command-V**.

Trackpad

Simple trackpad motions on your MacBook Air allow you to execute a multitude of tasks, like rotating photographs, zooming in on documents, and scrolling through webpages. Pressure-sensing features with the Force Touch trackpad create an additional layer of engagement. The trackpad offers feedback, so you can work more precisely. When you drag or rotate things, you feel a slight vibration when they're aligned.

Below are some of the common gestures;

Gestures	Action
Click Gesture Symbol	On the trackpad, press wherever. Alternatively, go to Trackpad Settings, activate "Tap to click," and just tap.
Force click gesture symbol	Press harder after clicking. Force-clicking a term to view its definition or an address to view a preview that you can open in Maps will allow you to look up more information.
Secondary click or right-click gesture symbol	Use two fingers to click to bring up shortcut menus. When "Tap to click" is activated, use two fingers to tap. Click the trackpad and hit the Control key on the keyboard.
Two-finger scroll gesture symbol	To scroll, move two fingers up or down.

Pinch to zoom gesture symbol	You can zoom in and out of pictures and webpages by pinching your thumb and finger open or closed.
Swipe to navigate the gesture symbol	Using two fingers, swipe left or right to navigate between web pages, and documents, and more like turning a page in a book.
Open launchpad symbol	Launch apps in Launchpad quickly. Use four or five fingers to pinch closed, and then touch an app to open it.
Switch between apps' gesture symbol	Use three or four fingers to swipe left or right to move between full-screen apps.

Try going into Trackpad Settings and changing the click pressure to a harder setting if you find yourself clicking by force when you don't mean to. Alternatively, switch the default setting for "Force Click with one finger" in the "Look up & data detectors" option to "Tap with three fingers."

Charge the battery

Every time your MacBook Air is linked to electricity, its battery is recharged.

- **Charge the battery**: Using the supplied connection and power adapter, link your MacBook Air to an electrical source.
- **Show battery status in the menu bar:** open the Battery options and click on your battery.

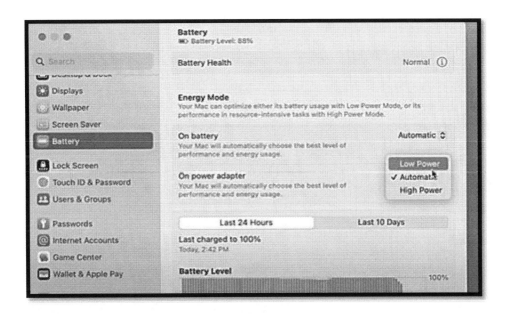

Click **Control Center in System Settings,** then selects **Battery on the right**, and lastly click **Show in Menu Bar.** The menu bar offers the option to display the battery % as well.

You can configure diverse choices for your battery in System Settings;

Optimized Battery Charging: By figuring out how often you charge your battery, this feature aids in extending its life and saving wear and tear. When it anticipates that you will be plugged in for a long time, it holds off on charging the battery past 80% in an attempt to finish charging it before you unplug.

- To enable Optimized Battery Charging, navigate to **System Settings,** select **Battery** from the sidebar, and click the **information icon next to Battery Health.**

Low Power Mode: This choice uses less energy. When traveling or spending a lot of time away from a power source, this is a wonderful solution. Select the Low Power Mode pop-up menu by clicking the **Battery icon in the sidebar of System Settings.**

Note: Click **Options in Battery Settings** to adjust other advanced settings, such as when to wake for network access, disable automatic sleeping, and dim the display when using a battery.

Connect the power adapter: Use a USB-C to MagSafe 3 cable attached to the power adapter or one of the Thunderbolt ports with a USB-C Charge Cable linked to the power adapter to charge the MacBook Air's battery.

Note: You may quickly charge the MacBook Air to 50% capacity in around 30 minutes by using the USB-C to MagSafe 3 Cable and the optional 70W USB-C Power Adapter.

Check the battery's charge: To view the battery level or charging status, look at the battery status icon located to the right of the menu bar. Alternatively, select **Battery in the sidebar of System Settings.**

Battery usage history: To view the battery usage for the previous 10 days or the last 24 hours, go to **System Settings** and select **Battery**.

Conserve battery power: You can decrease the brightness of the display, shut down programs, and unplug unused peripheral devices to increase the amount of time your battery lasts on a single charge. To adjust your power settings, select Battery from the sidebar of System Settings. When a device is attached to your MacBook Air while it is in sleep mode, the device's battery may discharge.

Adapters

You can link your MacBook Air to electrical power, external devices, screens, and more with the following Apple adapters.

- **USB-C to USB Adapter**: Link your MacBook Air to common USB devices.
- **USB-C to Lightning Cable**: To sync and charge your MacBook Air, connect your iPhone or any other iOS or iPadOS device.
- **USB-C AV Multiport Adapter**: In addition to attaching a USB-C charging cable and a conventional USB device, link your MacBook Air to an HDMI display to charge it.
- USB-C VGA Multiport Adapter: To charge your MacBook Air, connect it to a USB-C charging connection and a conventional USB device in addition to a VGA projector or monitor.
- Thunderbolt 3 (USB-C) to Thunderbolt 2 Adapter: Attach your MacBook Air to devices that support Thunderbolt 2.

Use Accessories

Your MacBook Air may be connected to a variety of additional gadgets, including wearable technology like AirPods and keyboards, mice, and trackpads. You can attach an accessory to your MacBook Air in two ways: either wirelessly via Bluetooth technology or by plugging the accessory's cable into a Thunderbolt 4 / USB-C or Thunderbolt / USB 4 connection.

Follow these steps before attaching an attachment to your MacBook Air:

- Refer to the instructions that were included in your attachment.
- Make sure you have the appropriate cable if you are connecting via one. To connect the connection to your MacBook Air's Thunderbolt / USB 4 connector, you might also require an adaptor.
- Ensure that the most recent macOS version is installed on your MacBook Air.

Connect a wireless accessory

Turn Bluetooth on: In the menu bar, select the Control Center icon. When Bluetooth is enabled, the symbol appears blue. Click the **gray icon to activate Bluetooth**.

Pair a Bluetooth accessory: You have to pair any Bluetooth accessories you want to utilize with your MacBook Air the first time. To ensure that your accessory is prepared for pairing, check the instructions that came with it. For example, you might need to flick a switch on the accessory to activate Bluetooth. The accessories and your Mac need to be close to one other and powered on. When the device is prepared for pairing, select Bluetooth from the sidebar when you launch System Preferences on your Mac. Click **Connect** after selecting the item from the list of nearby devices.

Connect a Bluetooth accessory: An accessory connects to your MacBook Air instantly once you've linked it. By selecting the Control Center icon from the menu bar, navigating to the Bluetooth device you have connected to your MacBook Air, and then clicking the arrow, you can see what devices are connected to it. Connected accessories are those that have a blue icon when they appear in the list.

If your device isn't connecting right away, click **Bluetooth in System Preferences** on your Mac. Verify that the attachment is listed among your devices. Follow the instructions to couple the accessory if it doesn't show up.

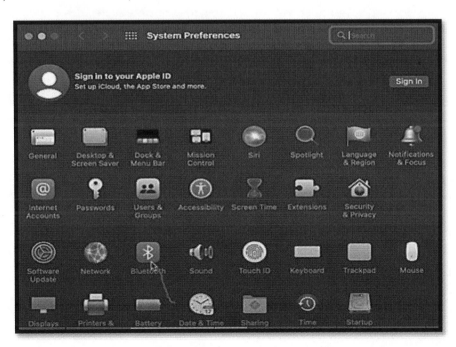

15

Disconnect or forget a Bluetooth accessory: Click **Bluetooth in System Settings** on your Mac to disconnect a Bluetooth device. Point your cursor over the attachment in the My Devices list, then select Disconnect. Click the Information symbol next to an item, and then select Forget This Device to prevent your MacBook Air from automatically connecting to it.

Connect a Magic Mouse, Magic Trackpad, or Magic Keyboard: Using the wire that came with your attachment, link the Magic Mouse, Magic Trackpad, or Magic Keyboard to your MacBook Air. Next, turn on your attachment by sliding its switch so that the green light appears. Next, pair your accessory with your Mac. You can use the attachment wirelessly after unplugging the cable and pairing it with your MacBook Air. When Bluetooth is enabled, your Mac and Magic Mouse, Magic Trackpad, or Magic Keyboard will instantly establish a connection.

Connect an accessory with a cable

You can use a cable to connect certain accessories to your MacBook Air. When connected, you might also be enabled to charge the accessory or send data, depending on the features of both the device and the cable. Before connecting, go to the instructions that come with your attachment. Certain attachments require an additional power source to be plugged in. You must use a cable that fits both the Thunderbolt / USB 4 port on your MacBook Air and the port on your accessory to connect an attachment. You can connect the cable with an adapter if it doesn't have the correct connector for your Mac.

Use an external display

You can utilize your MacBook Air with a projector, TV, or external display, such as the Apple Studio Display. Video output is supported by your MacBook Air's Thunderbolt / USB 4 connections.

Before you commence

Before connecting your display to the MacBook Air, be sure it is powered on.

- **Use the right cable for your display:** Verify the instructions that came with your display and confirm that the cable you are using to connect it is the right one.
- **Get familiar with the ports on your MacBook Air:** It's helpful to know what ports your MacBook Air has before you add a monitor to it.
- **Check technical specifications:** Examine your Technical Specifications to find out more about the types of displays that your MacBook Air is capable of supporting. Navigate to Display Support by opening **System Settings, and selecting Help > MacBook Air Specifications (you might have to scroll).**

Connect a display to the MacBook Air

One external monitor with a maximum of 6K resolution at 60 Hz or 4K resolution at 144 Hz is supported by your MacBook Air. Attach the display to a USB 4 or Thunderbolt port. When the laptop lid is closed, the MacBook Air with M3 processor supports up to two external screens, giving you even more workspace. Up to 6K resolution at 60 Hz or 4K resolution at 144 Hz can be displayed on the primary display, while up to 5K resolution at 60 Hz or 4K resolution at 100 Hz can be displayed on the secondary display. Assign the second Thunderbolt / USB 4 port to the second external monitor. You need to keep the lid closed, have the MacBook Air plugged in, and be linked to an external keyboard, mouse, and trackpad to utilize it with two external monitors.

Connect a display project to your MacBook Air

Your MacBook Air may be connected to a variety of monitors and projectors. If the connector on the display cable isn't compatible with the Thunderbolt / USB 4 ports on your MacBook Air, you can connect the display using an adapter (separately available).

- **USB-C display**: Attach the monitor to your MacBook Air's Thunderbolt or USB 4 connector.
- **HDMI display or TV**: To link your MacBook Air's Thunderbolt / USB 4 connector to an HDMI monitor or TV, use a USB-C Digital AV Multiport Adapter.
- **VGA display or project:** To connect the projector or display to a Thunderbolt / USB 4 port on your MacBook Air, use a USB-C VGA Multiport Adapter.

For further details and availability before making a purchase, go to apple.com, your neighborhood Apple Store, or other resellers. To make sure you select the correct product, go over the display's documentation or get in touch with the manufacturer.

After your display has been connected

Adjust and arrange displays

Once an external monitor or projector is connected, select displays from the sidebar by going to System Settings. From there, you may change the resolution and refresh rate (Hz), organize the displays, and decide which to use as your primary display. For optimal results, choose a lower resolution if you raise your display's refresh rate. The primary display is the one you connect first when connecting two monitors to your MacBook Air with an M3 processor. Disconnect them, and then rejoin in a different order to alter the main display. When you open the lid on your MacBook Air with an M3 chip and it has two displays connected, the laptop screen takes the place of the second monitor.

- Click the display you wish to use as a mirror, and then select **the mirror choice from the "Use as" menu to mirror your screen.**

Activity

- Charge the battery of your MacBook Air.
- What are the key features of the Magic Keyboard for MacBook Air?
- Use the Trackpad on your MacBook Air.
- What accessories can you use with your MacBook Air?
- Connect an external display to your MacBook Air.
- How can you customize the settings of the Magic Keyboard?
- What are some gestures you can use on the Trackpad?
- Check the battery health of your MacBook Air.
- What steps should you follow to use a USB-C accessory with your MacBook Air?

CHAPTER 2
GETTING STARTED

The MacBook laptops from Apple are among the greatest portable computers available. With the robust MacBook Pro and the portable MacBook Air, you can work or play wherever it's convenient for you. Included with every MacBook is macOS, the user-friendly operating system from Apple. This chapter explains how to turn on your MacBook, get around the macOS UI, and carry out some basic tasks.

Set up your Mac

You may transfer data from another computer, set up Touch ID, and change some Mac settings when you first set up your new MacBook Air. To set up your new Mac faster, you may also be able to skip a few steps and use your current settings if you already own a Mac, iPad, or iPhone. You can schedule an appointment at the Genius Bar, chat, email, or call an Apple specialist if you need more assistance setting up your Mac. To begin using your Mac, Setup Assistant guides you through the necessary configurations.

Set up your MacBook Air for new Mac users

The information provided is meant to be used in conjunction with Setup Assistant and covers every stage of the setup procedure. You may need to browse through some steps to choose an alternative. To navigate on a Mac, simply move your fingers up and down on the trackpad using two fingers.

Before you start;
- During setup, have your iPad or iPhone handy, as some steps might need confirmation on a different device.
- During setup, you have the option to move data from another computer, such as a Windows PC. Make sure the machine you wish to transfer data from has the most recent software version installed on it before you attempt this.
- It shouldn't take too long to set up your MacBook Air with the help of Setup Assistant. Set aside more time, though, if you decide to move data.

Set your language, country, or region, and connect to Wi-Fi

- **Choose your language**: Your Mac's language is set by doing this. Later on, to modify the language, go to **System Settings, select Language & Region from the sidebar, and then make your selections.**

- **Configure your country or region**: This configures your Mac's date format, currency, temperature, and other settings. Open **System Settings**, select **General from the sidebar**,

Click **Language & Region, and then make your selections.**

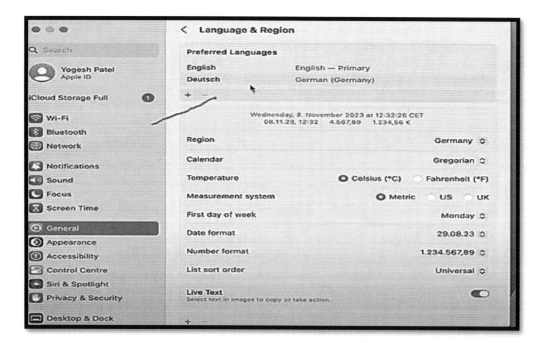

Turn on Accessibility features: Click **Not Now** to view accessibility options for motor, hearing, vision, and cognitive abilities. Press the Escape key on your keyboard to configure VoiceOver on your Mac. To see more accessibility options, you can also triple-click Touch ID, which is the top right button on your keyboard.

Connect to a Wi-Fi network: Select your **Wi-Fi network** and, if required, enter the password. You can also select **Other Network Options** and adhere to the onscreen instructions if you're using Ethernet. To connect the Ethernet cable to the MacBook Air's USB-C port, you'll need an additional Ethernet adapter, like the Belkin USB-C to Gigabit Ethernet Adapter. Open System Settings, select Wi-Fi from the sidebar, select a network, and if required, enter the password to modify the Wi-Fi network later.

Note: You might see a prompt to download the most recent macOS version during setup. Install as directed, and then carry out the remaining steps in the setup process.

Transfer information from another computer

You may transfer all of your data from a Windows computer to your new Mac, including files, contacts, accounts, and more. See Transfer information from another Mac if you would like to transfer from another Mac. Either wireless data transfer or an Ethernet cable connecting your Windows PC to your MacBook Air is the options available to you.

Before you commence;

Make sure the software on your Windows computer is updated to the most recent version. Then, on your Windows computer, download Migration Assistant.

Transfer data wirelessly

You need to connect your new Mac and Windows computer to the same wireless network. On the setup screen, click your Windows computer, and then adhere to the prompts.

Transfer data using an Ethernet cable

Use an Ethernet cable to connect your Mac directly to your Windows computer. To connect the cable to the USB-C port on your MacBook Air, you'll need an Ethernet adapter, like the Belkin USB-C to Gigabit Ethernet Adapter. Depending on its ports, you might want an adaptor to connect the Ethernet connection to your Windows computer. Once they are connected, click your Windows computer to see the setup screen, and then adhere to the prompts.

Sign in with Apple ID and set up your computer

You probably already have an Apple ID if you own another Apple product, such as an iPad or iPhone. You can create a free Apple ID right now if you don't already have one. A password and an email address make up your Apple ID. You use it for all activities on Apple, such as accessing iCloud, the Apple TV app, the App Store, and more. The username and password you use to access your Mac computer account are not the same as your Apple ID.

Do any of the following on the screen in the display;

- If you have an Apple ID, sign in with your password and email address. An iPhone or iPad that you own will receive a verification code. A verification code is texted to the phone number linked to your Apple ID if you don't own an iPhone or iPad. Follow the on-screen instructions if you don't get the text or the verification code.
- Click "**Create new Apple ID**" if you don't already have one.

- If your password or Apple ID is lost: Select **"Forgot password or Apple ID."**
- If, at this moment, you would prefer not to create or sign in using an Apple ID: Select **"Set up Later."** Following setup, you can use your existing Apple ID to log in or create a new one. Click "**Sign in with your Apple ID**" in the sidebar after opening System Settings.

Once done, **create a computer account**. Create **an account name and password after adding your name.**

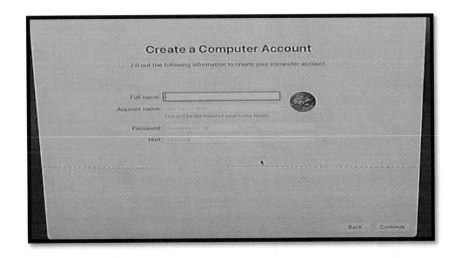

This will allow you to unlock your MacBook Air and authorize other actions. If you can't remember your computer account password, you can include an optional clue to help you get it back. Click **it to change your account's login image, and then select an alternative.** However, if you tick this option during setup, you can use your Apple ID to reset the password if you ever forget the one to unlock your Mac. Note: Your computer account and Apple ID are not the same.

Make this your new Mac

A screen for "Make This Your New Mac," which offers expedited setup, displays if you have already configured another device running iOS 15 or later or iPadOS 15 or later. This step is not visible to you if your iPad or iPhone does not have the latest software. (Are you unsure of the iPad or iPhone's software version? View Locate the iPod, iPad, or iPhone's software version.) By using the settings from your iCloud account, you may use Make This Your New Mac without having to go through multiple setup processes. Click **Continue** to use your current settings. Setup **Touch ID and Apple Pay** is the next step in the setup procedure.

Customize your Mac's privacy and security settings, turn on Screen Time, and enable Siri

Enable Location Services

Select which programs, including Maps, are allowed to use the location of your Mac. To modify your Location Services configuration at a later time, first visit **System Settings, select Privacy & Security from the sidebar**

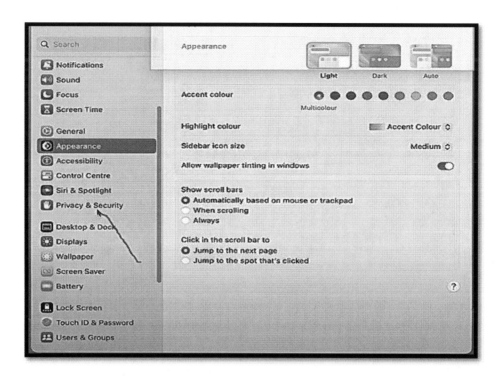

Then click Location Services and select your preferences.

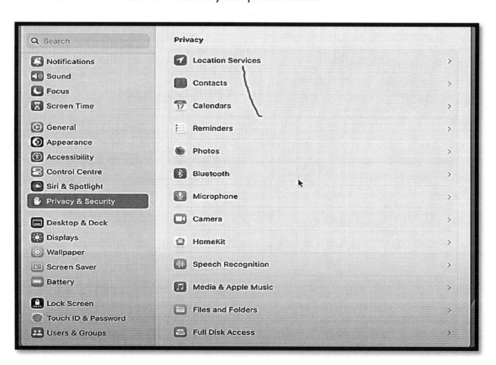

You are prompted to select your time zone if Location Services is not enabled.

Share analytics with Apple and Developers

Select whether to allow Apple to share crash and usage statistics with developers, as well as whether to transmit diagnostics and data to Apple. Open **System Settings, select Privacy & Security from the sidebar, then Analytics & Improvements (you might have to scroll), and select an option to modify these settings later.**

Set up Screen Time

With Screen Time, you can monitor how much time you spend on your MacBook Air every day and every week, regulate your kids' screen time, and set time limitations for using specific apps.

- Click **Continue to switch it on;** click **Set Up Later to turn it off**. To select your options if you decide to set up later, enter **System Settings and select Screen Time from the sidebar.**

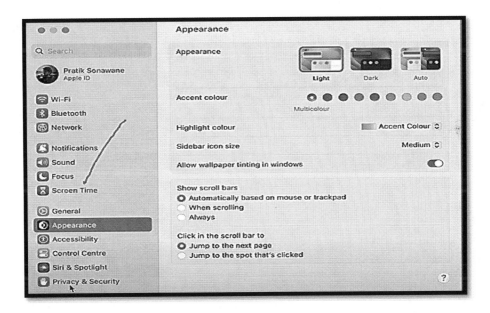

Secure your data with FileVault

FileVault contributes to the security of your data. You have the option to enable your iCloud account to access your disk if you forget your password, as well as to enable FileVault to safeguard your data during setup.

Enable Siri and Hey Siri

During setup, you can activate Siri and say "Hey Siri" to make your requests audible.

- Click **Enable Ask Siri to get started with Siri**. When prompted, speak multiple Siri instructions to set up "Hey Siri." Open System Settings, select **Siri & Spotlight from the sidebar** and make your selections to activate Siri and say "Hello Siri" later on.

To make Siri better during setup, you can also decide to share audio with Apple. Later on, you can always decide not to share the audio. Navigate to **Privacy & Security** in the sidebar of System Settings, select **Analytics & Improvements (you might have to scroll), and make your selections.**

Set up Touch ID and Apple Pay

Setting up Touch ID

During setup, you can add a fingerprint to Touch ID (the top-right button on your keyboard), which you can use to sign into some third-party apps, unlock your MacBook Air, and authorize purchases with Apple Pay. To set up Touch ID, follow the onscreen prompts.

- Select **Touch ID & Password in the sidebar after opening System Settings to set up Touch ID later or to add more fingerprints.**

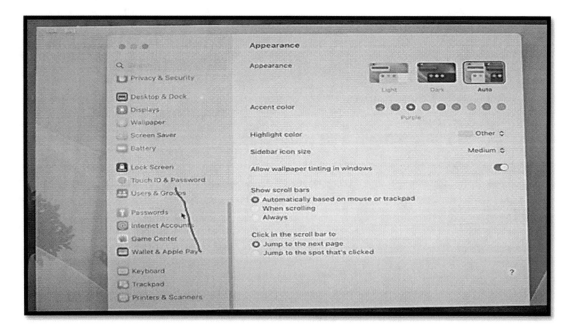

Hit the **Add button** and adhere to the on-screen directions to add a fingerprint.

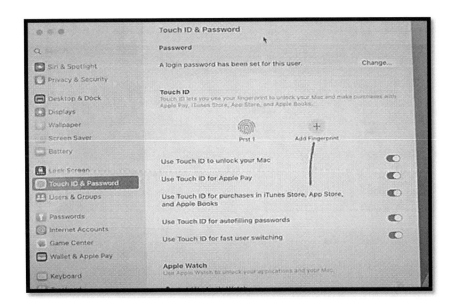

Set up Apple Pay

In addition to adding a debit, credit, or store card that may be used to make Touch ID purchases, setting up Touch ID also allows you to add Apple Pay. Enter your card information and adhere to the on-screen instructions. You may be asked to validate this card first if you currently use it to make media purchases.

- Click **Wallet & Apple Pay in System Settings to set up Apple Pay or add more cards later.** Observe the on-screen instructions to configure Apple Pay.

Note: The card issuer decides whether or not your card may be used with Apple Pay, and to finish the verification process, they might need more information from you. Apple Pay is compatible with a wide range of credit and debit cards.

Set desktop appearance

You can choose between Light, Dark, or Auto for your desktop theme. Later,

- Visit System Settings, click **Appearance, and choose an option if you want to reverse the setting decision you made.** Other visual options, like sidebar icon size and highlight color, are also configurable.

You can now begin customizing your MacBook Air once you've finished setting it up. Start personalizing your Mac by configuring your calendar and email accounts, resizing text and other elements on the screen, or changing the wallpaper on your desktop.

Apple ID and iCloud

Apple ID

You can use your Apple ID to log into any of your Apple services. Utilize your Apple ID to download apps from the App Store, access material from Apple TV, Apple Music, Apple Podcasts, and Apple Books, set up a Family Sharing group, and more. You can also use iCloud to keep your content updated across devices. You don't have to register for a new Apple ID if you misplace your password. To get your password back, simply click the **"Forgot Apple ID or password?"** option in the sign-in box. Make sure that every family member has their own Apple ID if other family members utilize Apple products. Your children can have Apple ID accounts, and you can use Family Sharing—which is covered later in this section—to share purchases and subscriptions. Handle every aspect of your Apple ID in one location. On your MacBook Air, open System Preferences. Family Sharing and your Apple ID are located at the top of the sidebar.

- Click "**Sign in with your Apple ID**" at the top of the sidebar to log in using your Apple ID, if you haven't already.
- Select your **Apple ID in the sidebar of System Settings**, and then choose an item to check and edit the data connected to your account.

Overview

Notifies you whether your account is set up and functioning well; if not, this is where you see tips and notifications.

Personal Information

Change the Memoji or photo linked to your Apple ID, along with your name and birthdate. You can also view how your data is maintained and configure your choices for communication with Apple.

Sign-In & Security

You can add or remove phone numbers and email addresses that you can use to log in, change the password for your Apple ID, enable two-factor authentication, and configure Account Recovery or Legacy Contact.

Payment and Shipping

Control the shipping address for items you buy from the Apple Store as well as the payment options connected to your Apple ID.

iCloud

After selecting which iCloud functions to enable, click **iCloud**. Additionally, you may control your iCloud storage and activate iCloud+ capabilities. Your content is saved in iCloud when you activate a feature, allowing you to view it from any device that has iCloud enabled and is signed in with the same Apple ID.

Use iCloud with your MacBook Air

You may collaborate with loved ones and keep your data current across all of your devices using iCloud. When you utilize iCloud and log in to all of your devices using the same Apple ID, your MacBook Air will work flawlessly with your iPhone, iPad, iPod touch, or Apple Watch.

- Click **"Sign in with your Apple ID"** in the sidebar after opening System Settings if you didn't activate iCloud when you originally set up your Mac. Once logged in, select **iCloud and toggle the iCloud functions on and off.**

Access your content across devices: To stay current, you can safely store, modify, and share your documents, images, and videos across devices with iCloud.

Use your MacBook Air with other devices: Use Continuity to transfer content between your MacBook Air and other devices with ease. Simply use your Apple ID to log in on each device, and your MacBook Air and other devices will conveniently cooperate when they are close to one another. For example, you can utilize your iPhone as a webcam for your MacBook Air, use AirPlay to stream your screen to another Mac or Apple TV, use Sidecar to arrange your iPad to work alongside your MacBook Air, and much more.

Do more with iCloud+: With the membership service iCloud+, you can save more files, images, and other content on your computer. Family Sharing allows you to share your iCloud+ storage plan. Custom email domains for your Mail address on iCloud.com, HomeKit Secure Video, and iCloud Private Relay are additional features of iCloud+.

Customize your Mac

System Settings on your Mac

You may personalize your MacBook Air and change its settings to fit your requirements by going into System Settings. You may, for instance, add a screensaver that doubles as your wallpaper, store and distribute passwords, use Display Settings to alter the brightness or resolution, tweak Accessibility settings, and much more. Downloading the most recent software update is also possible.

- To begin, click the **System Settings icon in the Dock or select System Settings from the Apple menu.** Next, **pick the desired setting in the sidebar.** You might have to scroll down to see all of the settings in the sidebar.

Lock your screen

After a certain amount of inactivity, you may configure your MacBook Air to either turn off the display or launch a screen saver. If you need to access the screen on your Mac again, you may also need to enter a password. Navigate to **Lock Screen under System Settings to configure.**

Choose a screen saver

Your MacBook Air display may become a work of art with slow-motion screensavers, which you can use as your wallpaper or while you're not using it. Open **System Preferences and select Screen Saver to configure.**

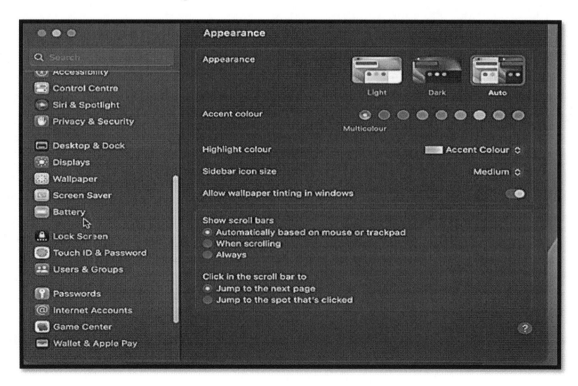

The screen savers that you select—Landscape, Cityscape, Underwater, Earth, or Shuffle Aerials—can also be set as your wallpaper by selecting the "**Show as wallpaper**" option.

Remember your passwords

Passwords that you keep in iCloud Keychain or on your Mac can be viewed in System Settings.

- After selecting **Passwords from the sidebar, login to your MacBook Air.** Click the information icon for the website you want to view your password for, then move your cursor over the password to see it. Moreover, you can click **the information icon to share it with AirDrop or update or remove it as a password.**

Share passwords and passkeys with others

Assemble a group of reliable contacts with access to the passkeys and passwords you wish to distribute. Your passkeys and passwords remain current even if you make modifications.

- Navigate to **System Preferences and select Passwords.** After selecting **New Shared Group** and giving the group a name, click the Add button and select Add People. Click **Add** once you've entered the names of the recipients you wish to share with. Choose the group, click the Add button, select Move Passwords to a Group, pick the accounts you wish to share, and then click Move to share passwords with the group.

Customize the Control Center and the menu bar

Select the settings you wish to show up in your menu bar or Control Center.

- Select **Control Center** from the sidebar of System Settings after making your selection.

Update macOS

To check if your Mac is running the most recent version of macOS software, select **General** from **System Settings and then click Software Update.** Software updates can be set up automatically.

Display settings for your Mac

Match the light in your surroundings

True Tone technology is built into your MacBook Air.

With True Tone, you can enjoy a more natural viewing experience by having the display automatically adjust its color to fit the light in your room.

- In the System Settings, turn on or off True Tone under the Displays section.

Use a dynamic desktop

When you use dynamic desktop wallpaper, it automatically adjusts to reflect the local time of day.

- In System Settings, click **Wallpaper**

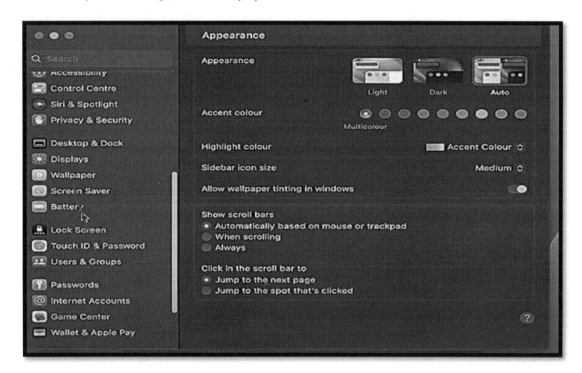

o **And select a picture to use for Dynamic Desktop.** Turn on **Location Services if you want your screen to adjust to your current time zone.** The image adjusts according to the time zone that is defined in the Date & Time settings if Location Services is disabled.

Alter how items show on the screen

To make anything on the screen larger, adjust the display resolution. You can also make text and icons larger to make them easier to view. A mouse shake can also help you rapidly locate or make the pointer easier to see.

Stay focused with Dark Mode

The Dock, menu bar, desktop, and all of the integrated macOS apps can all be customized with a dark color scheme. Darkened controls and windows fade into the background, allowing your content to take center stage. Apps like Mail, Contacts, Calendar, and Messages have white text on a black background, making it easier on the eyes when working in dimly lit areas. Professional photo editors will find that Dark Mode is perfectly calibrated—colors and subtle details contrast sharply with the dark app backgrounds. However, it's also fantastic for those who simply wish to concentrate on their content.

Night Shift

To lessen your exposure to harsh blue light, turn your Mac's color settings to warmer hues at night or in low light. Warmer screen colors could aid in improving your quality of sleep because blue light can make it more difficult to fall asleep. Night Shift can be programmed to switch on and off automatically at predetermined times, or it can be configured to turn on from dusk until dawn.

- Select **Displays from the System Settings menu, then click the Night Shift button at the bottom to customize your settings.** Change the color temperature by using the slider.

Screen Time on Mac

Screen Time lets you keep an eye on what your children are doing on their Apple devices, tracks how much time you spend on your MacBook Air, and offers features to make it simple to take a break during downtime.

See how you make use of your MacBook Air

See which apps notify you the most, how often you pick up your device each day, and how much time you spend using apps and websites in a given day or week by viewing reports.

- Click **System Preferences, select Screen Time from the sidebar, and then select Notifications, Pickups, and App & Website Activity.** Screen Time may need to be enabled before these options show up.

Set your limits

Establish time restrictions to manage the amount of time you spend using particular websites, applications, and app categories.

- Select **Downtime from Screen Time, enable Downtime, and then select the Schedule option from the pop-up menu to make a weekly schedule or a daily one.**

Manage the screen time of your kid

On their Mac, iPhone, or iPad, parents can set up Screen Time, and everything is ready for their children to use on their gadgets. The Books and Music applications allow you to set media ratings depending on age as well.

Don't miss the important things

- Select the websites or apps that you must always have access to. **Select Always Allowed under Screen Time, then activate the apps you want to be accessible while you're not working.**

Manage Windows on your Mac

It's not difficult to find yourself with a dozen open apps on your desktop, each with one or more windows. Fortunately, there are a few effective ways to see and use the open windows. You can select two apps to share the screen or enlarge one app to fill the entire screen when you wish to concentrate. Use Stage Manager to automatically arrange your windows and apps so you can switch between tasks quickly and maintain a clutter-free desktop. Use Mission Control to display all of your open windows in a single layer when you need to locate a window that is hidden. You can arrange your work across several computers and switch between them with ease by using multiple desktop spaces.

Use the whole screen

When you want your application to take up the entire screen, use a full-screen view. Numerous Mac apps, including Pages, Keynote, and Numbers, allow you to see content in full screen. When using full screen, you have the option to always see the menu bar or to hide it until you move the pointer over the top of the screen. When the pointer reaches the green button in the upper-left corner of the window,

- Select **Enter Full Screen from the menu that appears to enter or exit full-screen mode.**

Split the screen

When you use Split View, you can work in two app windows side by side. Just like the full screen, the two windows take up the entire screen.

- To use Split View, move the pointer over the green button located in the top-left corner of the window you want to use, then select **Tile Window to Left of Screen or Tile Window to Right of Screen** from the menu that appears. To use Split View, click on another window, and it will take up the other half of the screen automatically.

Stage Manager

Organize your windows and apps automatically to keep your desktop clutter-free. Your other windows should be situated on the side and click-accessible, with the focal area being front and center.

- Click **Stage Manager** after opening the Control Center.

Mission Control

Put all of your open windows into one layer quickly, and then click a window to put it back in front and make it active when you want to see the standard view again. Apps running in Split View or additional desktops (spaces) show up as a row at the top of the screen.

- Press the **Control-Up Arrow or the Mission Control key located on the upper row of your keyboard to enter or exit Mission Control. The Mission Control icon is another item you may add to the Dock.**

Widgets

Organize your desktop by arranging widgets from the widget gallery so you can quickly access your commonly used applications.

- To add, remove, or rearrange widgets, click **the date and time in the menu bar or Control-click the desktop.**

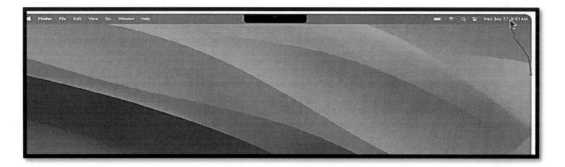

Then,

- Select **Edit Widgets**.

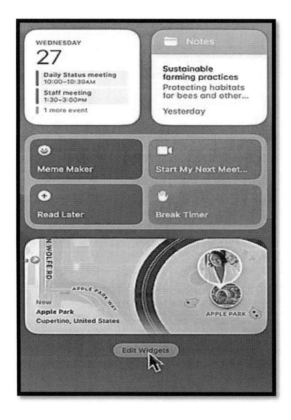

New widgets can be dragged to any location on your desktop or in the Notification Center. You may also bring your iPhone widgets on your desktop without installing the related Mac apps if you are logged in with the same Apple ID on both devices. Choose anywhere on the desktop wallpaper to swiftly move any open windows to the side if you want to see your desktop clearly when you have numerous windows open. When you're prepared to get back to work, click the **desktop wallpaper once more to bring up the Windows menu.**

When one desktop is not enough

As you work, switch between the various desktop locations that you have created for your app windows.

- Go into Mission Control and select the Add Desktop button to make a space.
- To navigate between your spaces, use **Mission Control and keyboard shortcuts.** As you work, you may add or remove spaces and drag windows from one area to another.

That horizontal traffic light

Every window has red, yellow, and green buttons in the top-left corner that are functional. To close an application window, click the **red button.** This dismisses all open windows and ends the program for some apps. Others experience the program remaining active while the current window is closed. The yellow button places the window on the right side of the **Dock and temporarily shuts it.** Click it in the Dock to expand it and open it again. Additionally, you may quickly switch between full-screen and split view in Windows by using the green button.

Connect with others

With the use of FaceTime and other video conferencing applications on your MacBook Air, you can establish connections with other people.

FaceTime

FaceTime allows you to have a conversation with an individual or a group of people on any device, no matter where you are—at home or away. Additionally, you may make and take calls directly from your MacBook Air via a Wi-Fi connection. Sending and receiving text messages is also possible.

- Make a FaceTime call: Make FaceTime video calls using your Mac's integrated FaceTime HD camera.
  - After selecting **New FaceTime and entering the recipient's name,** and **contact information (phone number or email address),** click FaceTime.

If making a video call isn't convenient, you can make an audio-only connection by clicking the pop-up menu and choosing FaceTime Audio. You have the option to join a FaceTime session using both audio and video when you receive an invitation.

- **Use FaceTime with a group**: In a group call, you can communicate with up to 32 individuals. Create a special link and distribute it to a group.
  - To create a link, click **Create Link**. You can either immediately share the link with others using Mail or Messages, or copy it to your Clipboard. On non-Apple devices, you can now join FaceTime calls via a link.
- **Set up FaceTime for phone calls**: Go to **Settings > Phone on your iPhone (iOS 9 or later) and turn on Wi-Fi calling**. Then launch FaceTime on your Mac. Select **General from the Settings menu**, then select "**Calls from iPhone.**"
- **Use FaceTime and Messages**: Send text messages from your MacBook Air using Messages. You can reply to texts from any of your devices—your MacBook Air, iPhone, iPad, iPod touch, and Apple Watch—by using Messages.

Add effects to your video conference

Select from a variety of video effects to improve your video conferencing experience when you use a compatible camera and an app that records video, like FaceTime. Note: Depending on the model of your Mac or the iPhone you're using as a webcam, you might only be able to use specific video effects.

- **Enhance your video**: Make changes to the lighting, background blur, and other video parameters. Select **an option for your camera, such as Portrait, Center Stage, or Studio Light, by clicking the Video button in the menu bar.**
- **React to the conversation**: Include a reaction that explodes hearts, confetti, fireworks, and other delightful 3D effects all over the camera frame. Select a

reaction by clicking the option next to Reactions after selecting the Video icon in the menu bar. Additionally, you can express a response with only a hand gesture. Verify that the green icon for Reactions is displayed.

- **Easily choose the screen you would like to share**: You can quickly share one or more apps from the window you are in when on a conversation using FaceTime or another compatible video conferencing app. Point your cursor over the Mission Control key located in the upper-left corner of your window, then select Share by clicking on the name of your videoconferencing program.
- **Overlay your video and your shared screen**: There are two overlays available: huge and mini. The small overlay places you in a movable bubble above your shared screen, but the large overlay keeps the focus on you by framing your screen next to you on a different layer. Select the **Large or Small option under Presenter Overlay after clicking the Video icon in the menu bar.**

Share experiences with SharePlay

You and your loved ones may watch TV shows and movies, listen to music, and see content together using SharePlay. On their iPhone (iOS 15 or later), iPad (iPadOS 15 or later), or Mac running macOS Monterey or later, your pals can take part. It is possible to watch material on Apple TV (tvOS 15 or later) and converse with friends on a different device at the same time.

Note: To participate in SharePlay, some apps need to be subscribed to. Not every country or area has access to every feature or piece of information.

- **Begin with using FaceTime**: To share an experience with friends, family, or coworkers, initiate a FaceTime call, invite them, and then utilize the SharePlay icon. Additionally, a SharePlay link can be added to a Messages thread.
- **Watch together**: Incorporate movies, TV series, online videos, and more into your group FaceTime conversations to foster relationships while you watch videos together. All players maintain sync even when you pause, rewind, fast-forward, or jump to a different scene. Smart volume allows you to communicate while watching by automatically adjusting the audio.
- **Listen together**: During FaceTime calls, you can play music for your pals or organize a full-fledged dance party. Any caller can add songs to the shared queue to listen to them together. Everyone on the call shares the playback settings, and you and the others can talk without raising your voices by listening at a smart volume.
- **Share your screen**: To include web pages, applications, and more in your FaceTime conversation, use SharePlay. You can include everything that shows on your screen in a shared moment. Explore vacation homes together, look through bridesmaid

clothes, impart a new skill, or present an unplanned photo presentation. You can share your entire screen or just one window.

Take a screenshot

To locate all the controls required for taking screenshots and screen recordings, navigate through the Screenshot menu. It's also possible to record your voice when you're screen recording. You may capture images and movies on your screen with the streamlined workflow, share, edit, and save them with ease.

Accessing the screenshot controls

Hit the Command-Shift-5 key. The screen as a whole, a single window, or a section of a window can all be captured. Additionally, you have the option to record the whole screen or just a specific area of it.

- To record your screen (Record Screen icon), capture **a selection (Capture Screen Selection icon), and do other operations, use the icons located at the bottom of the screen.** To change the location of your save, add a timer to start recording, adjust the microphone and audio settings, or display the pointer, click **Options**. To take a screenshot or record a video, click **Capture or Record.**

Mark up your screenshot

- To use Markup tools and annotate your screenshot, click **its thumbnail**. Right from the screenshot itself, you may share your marked-up screen with friends or coworkers by clicking the **Share icon.**

Backup, restore and transfer your data

Transfer Data

Your files and preferences can be moved to your new MacBook Air from an existing Mac or PC. You are prompted to transfer data from another computer when you first turn on your new MacBook Air.

Before you commence

- Update the operating system on both your new and old computers to the most recent version.
- Ensure that both computers are linked to the same network to transfer data wirelessly.

Transfer data from another Mac: Utilize Migration Assistant to move your data between your old and new devices via an Ethernet connection or over a wired or wireless network. Open a Finder window on both Macs, navigate to Applications, open the Utilities folder, double-click Migration Assistant, and then follow the prompts on the screen. If you are migrating wirelessly, keep the computers close to one another at all times.

Transfer data from a PC: For wired or wireless network data transfers, use Windows Migration Assistant.

Transfer data from a storage device: If a suitable adapter is required, link the storage item to your MacBook Air utilizing it.

Transfer data from a Time Machine backup: You can utilize Migration Assistant to restore data from a Time Machine backup if the hard drive of your old machine sustained damage.

Activity

- Change the battery on Mac?
- Set up a Mac for the first time?
- Configure Apple ID on a new Mac?
- Enable and use iCloud on Mac?
- What are the best methods to connect with others using a Mac?
- Take a screenshot on Mac?
- What are the steps to backup data on a Mac?
- How can I restore a Mac from a backup?
- Transfer data from an old Mac to a new one?

CHAPTER 3

USING MACBOOK AIR M3 WITH OTHER DEVICES

Share content between devices

Sharing content among Apple devices can be done in a variety of ways. To exchange files, images, passwords, and more, use AirDrop. Alternatively, use Universal Clipboard to copy and paste data between devices.

Share files and more with AirDrop

Sharing files with adjacent Mac, iPhone, iPad, and iPod touch devices is simple with AirDrop. The devices don't need to have the same Apple ID.

- Turn on AirDrop: In the menu bar, select the **Control Center icon**, and then select AirDrop. If you want to restrict who can AirDrop content to you, choose "Contacts only" or "Everyone."

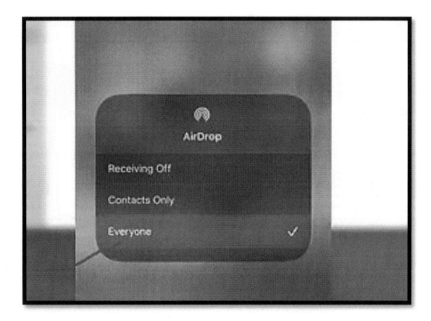

- Send a file from the Finder: To transmit an item, **control-click on it, pick Share > AirDrop, and then choose the device to send it to.** Alternatively, select **Go > AirDrop** or click the Finder icon in the Dock, followed by clicking AirDrop in the sidebar on the left.

Drag the file from the desktop or another Finder window to the person you wish to send it to when they show up in the window. The recipient of a file you provide them has the option of accepting it or rejecting it.

- **Send a file from an app**: Click the **Share button**

- o **Pick AirDrop**

o And then choose the device you want to transfer the item to while using an app like Pages or Preview.

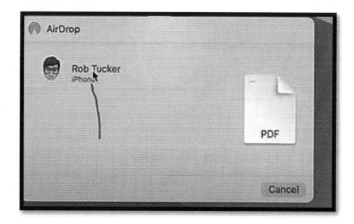

Make sure that both devices have Bluetooth and AirDrop enabled and are within 30 feet (9 meters) of one another if you are unable to see the recipient in the AirDrop window. Try selecting "Don't see who you're looking for?" if the recipient is using an older Mac.

- **Receive items using AirDrop**: You have the option to accept and save an item that someone sends to you on your Mac using AirDrop. If you want the item and receive the AirDrop message, click Accept. You may then save it to your Downloads folder or an app like Photos. You can send an item (such as an iPhone photo) from one device to another with ease and have it immediately saved if you have multiple devices logged in with the same iCloud account.

Stream content on a larger screen with AirPlay

You may send content from an iPhone, iPad, or even another Mac to your Mac using AirPlay, or you can use it to stream anything from your MacBook Air to a large screen. You have two options: either use your high-resolution TV as a second monitor or mirror the MacBook Air's screen onto it. Make sure your Apple TV and your MacBook Air are connected to the same Wi-Fi network to accomplish this. Additionally, you may play web videos straight on your high-definition TV without displaying anything from your desktop. This is useful if you want to watch a movie while keeping your work confidential.

Send content to your Mac from other devices

On your Mac, you can watch videos, listen to music, and do a lot more while your other devices are using them. Use your Mac as a secondary display for apps that support it, such as Keynote and Photos, to extend the display of your iPhone or iPad. You can use your Mac as a secondary speaker for multiroom audio or as an AirPlay 2 speaker to broadcast music or podcasts to your Mac. Any Apple device may be used with your Mac, and connecting the two is made considerably simpler if they have the same Apple ID.

Mirror your desktop with the use of Screen Mirroring

Select your **Apple TV by clicking the Control Center icon in the menu bar,** then selecting **Screen Mirroring.**

The symbol becomes blue when AirPlay is turned on.

Note: When an Apple TV is connected to the same network as your Mac and you have enabled AirPlay screen mirroring, you will notice an AirPlay status icon in the menu bar.

Play web videos without showing your desktop

Select your Apple TV by clicking the **Control Center icon** in the menu bar, then selecting **Screen Mirroring.** The symbol becomes blue when AirPlay is turned on. ote: When an Apple TV is connected to the same network as your Mac and you have enabled AirPlay screen mirroring, you will notice an AirPlay status icon in the menu bar.

Work with multiple devices

You can use your Mac with other Apple products. When you utilize your Mac, iPad, iPhone, or Apple Watch together, you can access amazing features thanks to Continuity.

Before you commence

Ensure that the iOS or iPadOS device and your MacBook Air are both signed in with the same Apple ID, have Bluetooth enabled, and have Wi-Fi switched on.

Using your iPhone with your Mac

Add iPhone widgets to your desktop: Immediately place your iPhone widgets on your Mac desktop. You can choose iPhone widgets for your Mac by using the Widget Gallery, or you can drag and drop Notification Center widgets onto your desktop. Control-click the desktop, and choose **Edit Widgets to launch the Widget Gallery.**

Use your iPhone as a webcam: You may use your iPhone as an extra camera for your Mac by using Continuity Camera on your Mac. You can record video calls with your iPhone's camera. Your Mac may automatically switch to using your iPhone as a camera when it is within range once you have configured Continuity Camera. If you would rather, a wired connection is also an option.

Note: An iPhone XR or later is needed to use Continuity Camera as a webcam. You must have iOS 12 or later on your iPhone or iPod touch, or iPadOS 13.1 or later on your iPad, to utilize Continuity Camera to share photographs.

Use your iPhone microphone: You can utilize your iPhone as a Mac's microphone by using Continuity Camera. During a video chat, you may choose to use your iPhone's microphone via the Video option in FaceTime or by going to the app's settings. You can also choose to utilize your iPhone as your system microphone by going to System Settings > Audio.

Phone calls and text messages on Mac: From your MacBook Air, you may make and receive calls using a Wi-Fi connection. Sending and receiving text messages is also possible.

To activate Wi-Fi calling on your iPhone, navigate to **Settings > Phone. Then launch FaceTime on your Mac**. Select General from the Settings menu, then select "Calls from iPhone."

Use your iPhone as a Hotspot: Have you lost your WiFi signal? With Instant Hotspot, you may rapidly connect your MacBook Air to the internet using the Personal Hotspot on your iPhone or iPad without entering a password.

In the menu bar, select the Wi-Fi status indicator. Next, select the Links icon that appears next to your iPhone or iPad in the list (click Other Networks if you don't see the list). The Links symbol replaces the Wi-Fi icon in the toolbar. On your device, there is nothing for you to do—the MacBook Air connects itself. To preserve battery life, your MacBook Air disconnects when you're not utilizing the hotspot.

Use your iPad with your Mac

Utilize your MacBook Air and iPad together to get even more out of it. With Sidecar, you can use your iPad as an additional display for your Mac, providing you more room to work with and utilize the Apple Pencil to draw in your favorite Mac programs. Transferring material between iPadOS and macOS is made simple using Universal Control, which allows you to operate your iPad with your Mac's keyboard, mouse, and trackpad. **Moreover, you can annotate PDFs, screenshots, and more rapidly.**

Use your iPad as another display for your Mac: You can use Sidecar to operate your iPad wirelessly up to 32 feet (10 meters) away from your Mac, or you may use a cable to connect your iPad to your Mac so that it can be charged. Go to the **Apple menu > System Settings, select Displays, and then select your iPad from the Add Monitor pop-up menu to configure it as a second monitor.** Afterwards, you may establish a connection with your iPad via the Control Center's Display section. In the Control Center, select the Sidecar button to unplug your iPad from your Mac. On your iPad, you can also tap the Disconnect symbol in the sidebar. **Note:** iPad models running iPadOS 13.1 (or later) and supporting the Apple Pencil can use Sidecar.

Set Sidecar settings: Navigate to Displays in System Settings, then choose your iPad's name. Next, you may customize your iPad's Sidecar settings, including whether it displays the sidebar and where it is, if it is the primary display or reflects your Mac, and whether you can double-tap with an Apple Pencil to access tools.

Note: These options are hidden from view in Display settings if your iPad has not yet been configured.

Use Apple Pencil: Draw and create precisely with your preferred professional programs. To use Apple Pencil on your iPad, simply drag the window from your Mac. Or an Apple Pencil to annotate screenshots, photos, and PDFs. **Note:** Only apps supporting the advanced stylus will function with pressure and tilt for the Apple Pencil.

Extend or mirror your desktop: You can drag and drop programs and documents between your Mac and iPad while your iPad is connected. It does this automatically by becoming an extension of your Mac desktop. To mirror the display and show your Mac screen on both devices, move your mouse over the Control Center Sidecar menu button, click the right arrow that appears above the button, and choose Mirror Built-in Retina Display. Open the menu and select Use As Separate Display to extend your desktop once more.

Take advantage of sidebar shortcuts: On your iPad, use the sidebar to rapidly access frequently used buttons and features. To use keyboard shortcuts, undo activities, and show or hide the Dock, menu bar, and keyboard, taps the buttons.

You can configure the Display settings to always show up in the menu bar for easy access to the Sidecar options. To choose whether to always have the Displays icon on the menu bar or only while it is active, navigate to **System Settings > Control Center.** From there, use the pop-up menu that appears next to Displays. The Sidecar menu button appears in place of the Display icon in the menu bar when Sidecar is enabled and your iPad is connected.

Use a single keyboard and mouse or trackpad to control multiple devices: You can control many devices with a single keyboard, mouse, and trackpad when you utilize Universal Control. To work across up to three devices, slide the pointer to the edge of your MacBook Air screen. It will then travel to your iPad or another Mac.

Note: You must be running macOS version 12.3 or later on your Mac and iPadOS 15.4 or later on your iPad to use Universal Control.

Check your connections: Your Mac's Universal Control connects to a device via Wi-Fi and uses Bluetooth to find other devices. Verify that every device is linked to Wi-Fi and has Bluetooth switched on. Additionally, confirm that Handoff is enabled in **Settings > General > AirPlay & Handoff on your iPad and in the General settings on your MacBook Air.** It is also required that you have enabled two-factor authentication and be logged in with the same Apple ID on both devices. You can connect your gadgets using the Control Center once these settings are accurate. Select a device beneath the **Link Keyboard and Mouse after selecting Control Center from the menu bar on your Mac.**

Move between screens: To bring the pointer on your Mac to the edge of the screen that is closest to your iPad, use your mouse or trackpad. Then, halt the movement of the pointer and move it a little bit beyond the edge. Continue dragging the pointer to the iPad screen until a border shows at the edge of the screen.

Drag and drop: Drag the text, picture, or other item you wish to move to the desired location on your other device after selecting it. For instance, you can drag an Apple Pencil drawing from your iPad into the Keynote application on your MacBook Air. It is also possible to copy content from one device to another and paste it there.

Share a keyboard: Start typing as soon as the pointer is in a document or anywhere else where text can be entered and the insertion point is blinking.

Activity

- Transfer files between my MacBook and iPhone?
- Mirror your MacBook screen to TV using AirPlay?
- Connect my MacBook to an external monitor.

CHAPTER 4

WHAT IS IN THE DESKTOP?

Menu bar

On a Mac, the menu bar extends across the top of the screen. The menu bar's menus and icons can be used to select commands, carry out tasks, and view status. It is possible to configure the menu bar to only appear when the pointer is moved to the top of the screen.

Apple menu

The top-left corner of the screen houses the Apple menu, which offers options for common tasks like updating programs, accessing System Preferences, locking your screen, and shutting down your Mac.

App menus

The Apple menu is adjacent to the app menus. The app name that you are currently using is bolded, and other menus with common names like File, Edit, Format, or Window follow. Every app includes a Help menu to make obtaining instructions on how to use the app simple. There are commands on every menu, most of which are common to most apps. For instance, the File menu frequently contains the Open command.

Status menus

Occasionally referred to as status menus, these items (usually shown as icons) can be found on the right end of the menu bar. They allow you to adjust features (such as keyboard brightness) or check the health of your Mac, including battery life. Click **an icon in the status menu** to view further information or options. To rapidly turn Wi-Fi on or off, for instance, click the Wi-Fi symbol and get a list of accessible networks. Which items appear in the menu bar is up to you to decide.

Spotlight

To search for objects on your Mac and the internet, click the **Spotlight symbol** if it appears in the menu bar.

Control Center

You can access frequently used functions like AirDrop, Stage Manager, Screen Mirroring, Focus, and more by clicking the **Control Center button**.

To the right of the Control Center are privacy indications, which can take the form of dots or arrows. The microphone on your Mac is in use when there is an orange dot next to the Control Center symbol in the menu bar; the camera is in use when there is a green dot; the system audio is being recorded when there is a purple dot; and the location is being used when there is an arrow. There is just one privacy indication dot displayed at once. For instance, you only see a green dot when the camera and microphone are both in use. There can be a field at the top of the Control Center that displays which apps are accessing your camera, microphone, location, or system audio. Clicking that field will open the Privacy box (macOS 13.3 or later), which may contain more information.

Notification Center

To access the Notification Center to browse widgets or catch up on missed notifications, click the date and time located at the right end of the menu bar.

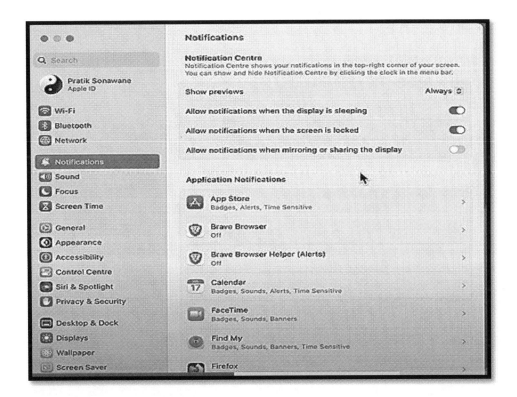

Work on the desktop

The Dock is located at the bottom of the screen, while the menu bar is at the top. The so-called desktop is located in between. All of your tasks are done on the desktop.

Change the desktop picture

You can use one of your pictures or select a different macOS desktop picture (dynamic ones change automatically during the day).

Change the desktop appearance

The appearance of the desktop image, Dock, menu bar, and built-in programs can all be changed from light to dark.

Use notifications on the desktop

Notifications about forthcoming events, incoming emails or messages, and other information show up in the top-right corner of your desktop screen. From the notification, you may request a reminder, respond to a message, and do a lot more. Notification timing and appearance are both customizable. Turn on a Focus to pause them for when you need to focus on anything specific.

Organize files on the desktop

Stacks are a useful tool for organizing files neatly by type or other criteria down one side of the desktop if you prefer to have files close at hand. New files are immediately added to a stack as they are added to the desktop.

Find a window on the desktop

If you have a lot of open windows on your desktop, you can use Mission Control to move them aside so you can see the desktop or to display a list of all the active windows so you can quickly find the window you need.

Use multiple desktops

To arrange tasks on particular desktops, you can make more desktop areas. For instance, you can quickly move between two desktops and use one to handle email while working on a project on another. Even each desktop can be tailored to fit the task you are working on.

Search with Spotlight

Spotlight is a useful tool for finding programs, documents, emails, and other Mac objects fast. You may also access news, stock prices, weather, sports scores, and more via Siri Suggestions. Even conversions and calculations can be handled by Spotlight.

Search for something

- Get any of the following done on your Mac;
  - In the menu bar, click **the Spotlight icon, if it is visible.**
  - Hit the **Command-Space bar.**
  - Press **on the keyboard's function key row, if available.**
- Enter your search term in the field; results will show as you enter. Top matches are listed first in Spotlight; click **one to preview or open it.** Additionally, Spotlight recommends different search terms; you can see these results online or in Spotlight.
- **Take up any of the following in the results displayed;**
  - View the outcomes of a recommended search in Spotlight: Select **an object that has the Spotlight icon before it.**

- View the outcomes of a recommended web search: After selecting an item, click the arrow icon.
- Access a piece of equipment: Give it two clicks. Alternatively, **pick the item and hit Return.**
- This operation could launch an application, including Help Viewer, Messages, and others.
- Perform a quick action: You might be able to perform a quick action, such as writing an email or placing a FaceTime call when you type a phone number, email, date, or time.
- Display a file's location on your Mac: After choosing the file, hold down the Command key. The location of the file is shown at the preview's bottom.
- Make a copy of something: You can drag a file into a Finder window or the desktop.
- Toggle a setting on or off: When you look for a setting in Spotlight, click to toggle it on or off (for example, VoiceOver).

App icons in results are dimmed and an hourglass indicator appears when there is a pause in service or when you exceed the time limit configured for apps in the Screen Time settings.

Get calculations and conversions in Spotlight

In the Spotlight search field, you can type in a mathematical expression, a currency amount, a temperature, and more to get a conversion or computation in the same spot.

- **Calculations:** Type in a mathematical expression, such as 2020/15 or 956*23.94.
- **Conversions of currencies**: Type in a sum of money, like $100, 100 yen, or "300 krone in euros."
- **Converting temperatures**: Type in a value, such as 32C, 98.8F, or "340K in F."
- **Convert measurements**: Type in a measurement, like 25 pounds, 54 yards, 23 stone, or "32 feet to meters."
- **World clock conversions**: Type in a statement describing the time in a certain location, like "local time in Japan" or "time in Paris."

Certain disks, folders, or information kinds (such as emails or messages) can be added or removed from Spotlight searches. You may disable Siri Suggestions for Spotlight if you want it to exclusively search information on your Mac and exclude results from the internet.

Quickly change settings

You can quickly access important macOS settings, like AirDrop, Wi-Fi, and Focus, with Control Center on Mac. Additional features, such as battery status, quick user switching, and accessibility shortcuts, can be added to the Control Center through customization.

Using the Control Center

- Choose the Control Center in the menu bar.
- Get any of the following done in the Control Center;
  - Drag a slider to change a setting's value; on your Mac, for instance, drag the Sound slider to change the level.
  - To activate or deactivate a function, click its symbol; for example, click **AirDrop or Bluetooth®.**
  - To view further options, click an item (or its arrow). For instance, click **Focus to view your Focus list and enable or disable a focus**

  - Or click Screen Mirroring to select a target display.

You can drag an item from the Control Center to the menu bar if you use it frequently so you can always have it accessible. Holding down the **Command key while dragging the item out of the menu bar will remove it from the bar.**

Customize Control Center

Select System Preferences from the Apple menu on your Mac, and then click **Control Center** from the sidebar. (You might have to scroll below.) The things in these categories on the right have settings that you can select.

- **Control Center Modules**: You cannot remove the items in this section; they are always displayed in the Control Center. It is also an option to display them on the menu bar. Select an option by clicking the pop-up menu that appears next to the item.
- **Other Modules**: The items in this section can be added to the menu bar and Control Center. Toggle on or off each of the options below an item. There might be more settings available for some goods.
- **Menu Bar Only:** In addition to adding other elements (such as Time Machine, Siri, Spotlight, and VPN status) to the menu bar, you may customize the menu bar clock.

Use Siri

On your Mac, you may use Siri to accomplish routine things like scheduling a meeting, launching an application, or finding prompt answers to inquiries.

Turn on Siri

- Select **System Settings from the Apple menu** on your Mac, then select **Siri & Spotlight** from the sidebar. (You might have to scroll below.)

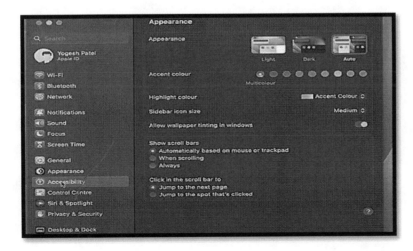

- If Ask Siri isn't currently on, switch it on on the right by clicking **Enable.**
  You are prompted to enable Siri if you attempt to use it while the option isn't enabled. To utilize Siri, you need to have an internet connection.
- **When prompted to enhance Siri and Dictation, choose from the following actions:**
  - Share audio recordings: To permit Apple to record the sound of your Mac Siri and Dictation interactions, click **Share Audio Recordings.** An example of stored audio may be reviewed by Apple.
  - Do not distribute audio recordings: Select "**Not Now.**"

If you decide later on to share or not share audio recordings, go to System Settings from the Apple menu, then select Privacy & Security from the sidebar. (You might have to scroll below.) Toggle the Improve Siri & Dictation option on or off by clicking Analytics & Improvements on the right. Note: You are free to remove the audio interactions at any time. They are under six months old and are linked to a random identifier.

- **Get any of the following done;**
  - Use "Hey Siri" or "Siri": To use Siri, turn on the "Listen for" option or select the phrase you want to utter, if it is available for your device and language.

You can use Siri when your Mac is locked or in sleep mode if you choose "**Allow Siri when locked**" **and this option is enabled.**
  - Configure a keyboard shortcut: To launch Siri, click the **"Keyboard shortcut"** pop-up menu, select one, or make your own.

- ○ **Choose how Siri speaks:** Select a language by clicking the Language pop-up menu. After selecting your preferred voice from the Voice Variety and Siri Voice choices, click **Select next to "Siri voice" to hear a preview.** (There can be just one option in some languages.)
- ○ **Mute Siri:** To stop Siri from speaking, click Siri Responses and then off "Voice feedback." Siri will respond, but it will only display in the Siri window.

Select **Siri Suggestions & Privacy, followed by About Siri & Privacy** to find out more about how Apple safeguards your data and gives you control over what you share. Select **Apple menu > System Settings**, then select **Control Center** in the sidebar to add Siri to the menu bar. (You might have to scroll below.) Select Show in Menu Bar next to Siri after selecting Menu Bar Only on the right.

Activate Siri

Note that for you to be able to make use of Siri, you must be connected to the internet.
- **Do any of the below instructions to get Siri activated;**
  - ○ Use the keyboard shortcut that is indicated in the Siri & Spotlight settings, or press and hold the Microphone key if it is present in the row of function keys.
  - ○ Within the menu bar, select Siri. You can add it utilizing Control Center settings if it's not displayed.
  - ○ If your Mac has a **Touch Bar, tap Siri in the Touch Bar.**
  - ○ Say "Hey Siri" or "Siri" (if the Siri & Spotlight settings allow you to do so).
- Make a request, such as "What was the score for the game last night?" or "Set up a meeting at 9." Your device's location will be ascertained at the moment you submit a request if you have enabled Location Services. Under **System Settings, you can modify this setting.**

Switch off Siri

- Select System Settings from the Apple menu on your Mac, and then select Siri & Spotlight from the sidebar. (You might have to scroll below.)
- Toggle off **Ask Siri on the right.**

You can limit a child's access to Siri & Dictation and set up Screen Time for them if you're the family organizer for a Family Sharing group.

Notifications: You can track missed alerts in the Notification Center on your Mac, as well as utilize widgets to see appointments, birthdays, the weather, top stories, and more directly from the desktop.

Open or close the Notification Center on your Mac

Do any of the following on your Mac;
- **Open Notification Center**: Either swipe left using two fingers from the trackpad's right edge, or select the date and time in the menu bar.
- **Close Notification Center**: You have three options: click wherever on the desktop, select the date and time in the menu bar, or use two fingers to swipe right toward the trackpad's right side.

Use notifications in the Notification Center on your Mac

In the Notification Center, drag the pointer over any notification and then do any of the following;
- Stacks of notifications can be expanded or collapsed. When notifications in an app are grouped, they are stacked. Click anywhere in the top notice to expand the stack and view all of the alerts. To make the stack smaller, select "**Show less.**"
- Act now: Press the button. For instance, select **Snooze from a Calendar app notice or Reply from a Mail app notification**. Click the arrow for additional options if there is one next to an action. For instance, in the Messages app, select **the arrow next to Decline** and select **Reply with Message to respond to a call.**
- View other information: To view the item in the app, click **the notification.** To view details in the notice, click **the arrow if it appears to the right of the app name.**
- Modify an application's notification settings by clicking the arrow that appears to the right of the app name, selecting Notifications from the menu, and then selecting **Mute or Turn Off from there.**
- Either removes a single notification or the entire stack of notifications: Select the **option to Clear or Clear All.**

Use widgets in the Notification Center on your Mac

Perform any of the following actions in the Notification Center:
- View other information: Anywhere in a widget can be clicked to launch the associated webpage, program, or settings. For instance, click the **Weather widget to launch the Weather app and view the entire forecast, or click the Reminders widget to enter the Reminders app.**
- To resize a widget, select **a widget by doing a control-click and adjusting its size.**
- To remove a widget, slide the pointer over it while holding down **the Option key,** and finally hit the **Remove button.**

Notification Center widgets can be customized and the widgets that are displayed can be changed. Use a Focus, like Do Not Disturb or Work, to reduce distractions by shutting off all notifications or letting only specific notifications show up.

Opening apps from the Dock

On the Mac desktop, the Dock provides easy access to frequently used applications and features, like Launchpad and Trash. In addition to a folder containing stuff you download from the internet, the Dock can display up to three recently used programs that are not already in it. The Dock appears at the bottom of the screen by default, but you may choose to have it show along the left or right border.

Open items in the Dock

Choose from the following options in your Mac's Dock:

- To open an application, click its icon. Click the **Finder icon on the Dock, for instance, to launch the Finder.**

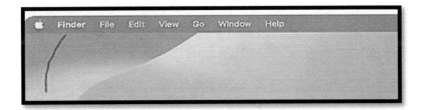

- Get a file opened in an app: Over an app's icon, drag the file. Drag the document over the Pages icon in the Dock, for instance, to open a document you produced in Pages.
- Display a file in the Finder: Press **and hold the item's icon**.
- Conceal the current app and open the prior one: Choose the icon of the open application.
- Hide every other app and move to another one: To switch between apps, **press and hold the icon of the desired app.**

Take other actions for items in the Dock

Choose one of the following actions from the Mac's Dock:

- **Show an action shortcut menu**: To view an item's shortcut menu, control-click it. From there, select an action (like Show Recents) or click a filename to open the file.

- To stop an app from responding, Control-click its icon and select **Force Quit** (you might lose any saved changes).

Add, remove, or rearrange Dock items

Try any of the following options on your Mac:
- **Put something in the Dock**: Move the apps to the left of the recently used app separation line, or even above it. Move files and folders beneath the line dividing recently used apps, or to the right of it. The object has an alias that is put in the Dock.
- To take away something from the Dock, drag it out until the **Remove option appears**. The real thing is still on your Mac; only the alias gets deleted. It's simple to restore an app icon from the Dock if you unintentionally delete it (the software remains on your Mac). To get the app's icon back in the Dock, open it. Click **the app's icon with the control key**, then select **Options > Keep in Dock**.
- Organize objects in the Dock by dragging them to a different spot.

Customize the Dock

- Select **System Settings** from the Apple menu on your Mac, and then select Desktop & Dock from the sidebar. (You might have to scroll below.)

- Make the desired changes to the options below Dock on the right. You can, for instance, alter the Dock's appearance, size, and location relative to the left or right border of the screen, or even make it invisible.
- Click the **Help button** at the lower part of the window to see the available options.

Drag the pointer over the borderline in the Dock until a double arrow shows up, then click and drag the pointer down or up to swiftly change the size of the Dock. To access more shortcut menu actions, control-click the divider. Keyboard shortcuts are another way to access the Dock. Fn-Control-F3 will take you to the Dock. Then navigate between icons using the Left and Right Arrow keys. When an item is open, press Return. You need to perform one or more actions in an app or System Settings when you see a red badge on an icon in the Dock. You have new emails to read, for instance, when you see a red badge on the Mail symbol in the Dock.

Organize your files in the Finder

The center of your Mac is the Finder. Clicking the Finder icon in the Dock will launch a Finder window; the icon resembles a blue happy face. **Nearly everything on your Mac can be accessed and organized using Finder windows.**

- **See your stuff**: Click on objects to view your downloads, programs, files, and more in the Finder sidebar. Customize the sidebar to increase its usefulness even further. Show the Preview pane to add even more functionality to the Finder window.
- **Access everything, everywhere**: To store files and folders in iCloud, use iCloud Drive. Any device that has your same Apple ID signed in allows you to access them.
- **Clean a messy desktop**: Stacks facilitate file organization on the desktop by grouping files neatly. Stacks can be categorized by kind, date, or tags. Sorting your photographs into stacks, presentations into stacks, and so forth happens when you organize by kind. When you add new files, they are automatically added to the appropriate stack, which helps you maintain organization.
- **Choose your view**: You have a choice in how Finder windows display items. For instance, Gallery View allows you to visually browse through your files and folders instead of having to see your stuff as a list.
- **Send files or folders**: Right from the Finder, you may copy a file or folder to a nearby Mac, iPhone, or iPad. To begin, click AirDrop in the sidebar. Additionally, you may choose a file or folder in the Finder, and then transfer it via Mail, AirDrop, Messages, and other services by clicking the Share button or using the Touch Bar. Select the More Toolbar Items button at the end of the toolbar if the Share button isn't visible.
- **Share files or folders**: iCloud Drive allows you to collaborate on a file or folder with other iCloud users. To begin, choose Share File or Share Folder after selecting a file

or folder in the Finder and clicking the Share button (or using the Touch Bar). Select the More Toolbar Items icon at the end of the toolbar if the Share button isn't visible.

- Click the **iCloud Drive folder** in the sidebar to view all of your documents saved there.
- Click the Shared folder to view only the papers that you have been invited to collaborate on, that you are sharing, and that are shared with you. To modify the contents displayed in the sidebar, select **Finder > Settings.**

Sync information between your Mac and other devices

Your Mac and iPhone, iPad, or iPod touch can be connected to exchange and update data. Once you add a video to your Mac, for instance, you may watch it on both devices by syncing it with your iPhone. Books, podcasts, TV series, music, movies, and more can all be synced.

Activity

- Customize the Menu bar on MacBook
- Organizing a desktop?
- Use Spotlight to find files and applications quickly
- Adjust system settings on my MacBook
- Activate and use Siri on my MacBook
- Manage and prioritize notifications effectively
- Add or remove apps from the Dock?
- Organize files and folders in the Finder

CHAPTER 5

THE BASICS

Connect to the internet

Whether you're at home, at work, or on the go, your Mac can connect you to the internet. Using an Ethernet (wired) or Wi-Fi (wireless) connection are the two most popular methods to access the internet. If neither is accessible, an Instant Hotspot might work.

Use Wi-Fi

The Wi-Fi icon appears in the menu bar at the top of the screen when there is a Wi-Fi network accessible. After selecting a network to join, click the symbol. If the network name has a lock icon next to it, the network is password-protected; you must input the password to access the Wi-Fi network.

Use Ethernet

Ethernet can be used via DSL or cable modems, Ethernet networks, or both. If Ethernet is supported, attach an Ethernet cable to your Mac's Ethernet port, which is denoted by this symbol. You can connect the Ethernet cable to your Mac's USB or Thunderbolt port using an adapter if it doesn't have an Ethernet port built-in.

Use Instant Hotspot

Using the personal hotspot on your iPhone or iPad, you might be able to utilize your Mac and Instant Hotspot to connect to the internet if you don't have access to Wi-Fi or an Ethernet connection.

At home, at work, or on the go

In your home: Wi-Fi or Ethernet internet connections may be provided by your ISP. If you're unsure about the kind of access you have, ask your ISP. You might have access to an Ethernet or Wi-Fi network connection at work. For information on usage guidelines and instructions on connecting to your business network, get in touch with the network administrator or IT department of your organization. When you're on the go, you can use Instant Hotspot on your Mac (if both your Mac and your phone carrier support it) or Wi-Fi hotspots, which are public wireless networks. Remember that to access certain Wi-Fi hotspots, you may need to pay a price, agree to terms of service, or enter a password.

Browse the web

You can find nearly anything on the internet by using Safari on your Mac to visit websites. This is the way to get going.

Search for information

Almost anything can be searched for on the internet using the Smart Search area located at the top of the Safari window. Type in your query, such as "ice cream near me," then select from the list of suggested searches that appear.

Go to a website

To access a website, you can also use the Smart Search box located at the top of the Safari window. Simply type the website's address or name.

Choose a homepage

You can set a website as your homepage so that it opens in a new Safari window if you like to visit it frequently.

- Select **Safari > Settings**, click **General**, and type the address of the website (or select the webpage you are now viewing by clicking **Set to Current Page**).

Bookmark websites

You can simply revisit websites you bookmark if you find ones you wish to view again.

- Select **Add Bookmark** after clicking the Share icon in the toolbar.
- Click the **Sidebar** button in the toolbar, followed by the **Bookmarks** button, to access a bookmarked webpage.

Preview a file

Almost any type of file may be quickly and fully seen without opening it using Quick Look. Within the Quick Look window, you may directly rotate photographs, trim audio and video clips, and use Markup.

- Tap the Spacebar after selecting one or more things on your Mac. A window for Quick Look opens. The last item you choose is displayed first if you picked more than one.
- In the Quick Look window, get any of the following done;
  - **Resize the window**: The Quick Look window's upper-left corner contains the Full Screen button. Click the **Exit Full-Screen button** that displays after moving the pointer to the bottom of the window to end full-screen mode.
  - **Zoom in and out of an item**: To zoom in or out of an object, use Command-Plus (+) to enlarge the image or Command-Minus (–) to reduce it.
  - **Rotate an item**: To rotate an object, either hit and hold the Option key, then click the **Rotate Left button, or click the Rotate Right button**. To keep the thing revolving, click again.
  - **Trim an audio or video item**: To trim a piece of audio or video, click the Trim button and drag the trimming bar's yellow handles. Click **Play** to see how your changes look. Click Revert to start afresh. When you're prepared to

save your modifications, select whether to overwrite the current file or to create a new one by clicking Done.

- ○ **Browse items:** Examine the items (should you have chosen more than one): Press the Left or Right Arrow keys, or use the arrows located in the upper-left corner of the window. To view the items as a slideshow, click the Play button to view them in full screen.
- ○ **Display items in a grid:** If more than one item was selected, display the items in a grid: Use the Command-Return key or click the Index Sheet button.
- ○ **Share an item:** Choose the Share button and then select just how you would like to get them shared.
- ○ **Copy the subject of an item:** If the object is a screenshot or picture, you can remove the background and focus only on the picture's subject. Control-click on the picture and select Copy Subject. The subject can now be pasted into a note, email, text message, or document.
- Once you're done, shut the Quick Look window by clicking the **Close button or using the Spacebar.**

The video element of a Live Photo automatically starts to play when you access it in the Quick Look window. Select Live Photo in the lower-left corner of the image to view it again.

Alter your display brightness

The brightness of the display can be changed either manually or automatically.

Use the brightness function keys

You can change the brightness of your display if it appears too bright or too dark.

- Press the **up** or **down** arrow keys on your Mac to adjust the brightness (or use the Control Strip).

Instantly adjust brightness

- Click **Displays** in the sidebar after selecting **Apple menu** > **System Settings** if your Mac has an ambient light sensor. (You might have to scroll below.)

- On the right, select **"Automatically adjust brightness."**

- You can manually change the brightness if you don't see the "Automatically adjust brightness" option.

Manually modify brightness

- Select **System Settings** from the Apple menu on your Mac, then click **Displays from the sidebar. (You might have to scroll below.)**

To change the brightness of your display, drag the **Brightness slider to the right.**

Modify the volume

You can use any of the following to adjust the volume on your Mac:
- Use the **Control Strip** or the keyboard's volume keys. For instance, tap to instantly mute the volume.
- To change the volume, click the **Sound control in the Control Center or menu bar and drag the slider.**

Note: Select **Apple menu > System Settings,** then select **Control Center** in the sidebar if the Sound control isn't in the menu bar. (You might have to scroll below.) To display Sound in the menu bar always or only when it's active, click the pop-up menu that appears next to Sound on the right.
- Utilize the app's volume controls, such as the Apple TV app.

Adjust the volume of Music on the Mac

You have the option to adjust the volume for each song, for each song individually, or to have all songs play at the same volume. You can use other speakers, like a HomePod or Bluetooth® speakers, to listen to music in the Music app in addition to the built-in speakers on your computer.

- You can listen to internet broadcasts, play CDs, stream music from Apple Music, play Apple Music radio, or play music from your library using the Mac's Music program.
- **You can use any of the following to adjust the volume:**
  - Adjust the level for every song (just like you would on a stereo): Utilize the Music window's volume slider, located near the top.
  - Volume-adjust a certain song or music video: Click Options, select **Song > Info, and then drag the volume slider.**
  - Make sure that the loudness of all songs and music videos is always the same: Click **Playback under Music > Settings, then choose Sound Check.**
- Click the **AirPlay button and choose the checkbox next to the speaker to use speakers other than the built-in ones.** The following speaker kinds are supported:

Change the sound output settings on the Mac

The built-in speakers on your Mac, the speakers on your display (if it has speakers), speakers, headphones, or other devices that are connected to your Mac or that are accessible wirelessly via AirPlay can all be used to play music.

- Select **System Settings from the Apple menu on your Mac, then select Sound from the sidebar. (You might have to scroll below.)**
- To choose the desired device from the list of sound output devices, click the **Output button on the right.**
  - The built-in speakers on your Mac, devices plugged into the sound port (Audio port icon), USB speakers, and AirPlay devices are all shown as sound output devices that you can use.
  - Select Headphones for any device that is connected to the computer's audio port.
- **Go get your sound output settings adjusted, and get any of the following done;**
  - **Turn up the volume**: Move the slider for output volume.
  - You can adjust the volume from anywhere if Sound is enabled in the menu bar.
  - Drag the Alert volume slider in Sound Effects to adjust the loudness of alert noises. Because the alarm volume is based on the loudness of your

computer, lowering the computer's volume will also result in a quieter alert sound.

- ○ **Cut off the sound output**: Check the box labeled "Mute."
- ○ **Modify the balance**: Slide the Balance slider.

Applications with volume controls, like Music or iMovie, can only have their settings equal to or lower than the output volume of the machine. They don't take precedence over your Sound settings selections.

Use trackpad and mouse gestures

You can utilize gestures, such as click, **tap, squeeze, and swipe,** to zoom in on documents, navigate through music or webpages, rotate photographs, launch Notification Center, and more when you use an Apple trackpad or Magic Mouse with your Mac.

Trackpad gestures

To click, tap, slide, swipe, and perform other actions on your trackpad, place one or more fingers on its surface. For instance, you can use two fingers to swipe left or right to navigate between pages in a document.

- Select **Apple menu > System Settings, then select Trackpad** in the sidebar to see the trackpad gestures that you can use on your Mac, along with a short video that walks you through each motion. (You might have to scroll below.)

Within the Trackpad settings, gestures can also be customized or turned off.

Mouse gestures

You can click, tap, slide, or swipe objects on your mouse by placing one or more fingers on its surface. For instance, you can use one finger to swipe left or right to flip between pages in a document.

- Select **Apple menu > System Settings, then Tap Mouse** in the sidebar to see the mouse movements that you can use on your Mac, along with a short video that walks you through each gesture. (You might have to scroll below.)

Gestures can also be customized or turned off in the Mouse options.

Change Trackpad settings on Mac

To modify the functionality of your trackpad on your Mac, go to the Trackpad settings. You may alter the speed at which the onscreen pointer moves when you drag your finger across the trackpad, for instance, and you can personalize the movements that you use with it.

Note: You may only see part of the options listed below, depending on the type of Mac you are using.

- To modify these configurations, select **System Settings from the Apple menu, then select Trackpad from the sidebar. (You might have to scroll below.)**

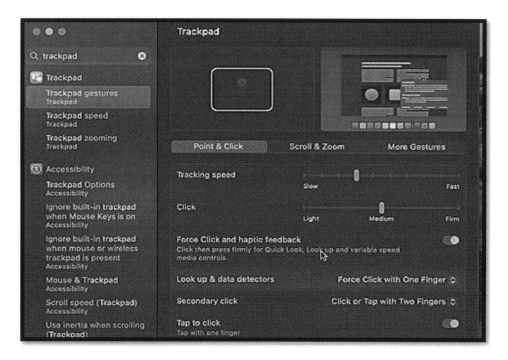

Use Touch ID

You can use Touch ID on your Mac or Magic Keyboard to unlock your computer, approve purchases from iTunes, App Store, and Apple Books, and utilize Apple Pay to make online transactions. Additionally, Touch ID may be used to log into certain third-party apps.

Set up Touch ID

- Select **System Settings** from the Apple menu on your Mac, and then select **Touch ID & Password on the sidebar. (You might have to scroll below.)**
- After selecting **Add Fingerprint and entering your password**, adhere to the on-screen directions. The Touch ID sensor is situated in the upper right corner of your keyboard if your Mac or Magic Keyboard has one. Your user account can have up to three fingerprints added to it (up to five fingerprints saved on your Mac).
- Choose how you would like to make use of the Touch ID;
  - To unlock your Mac after waking it up from sleep, use **Touch ID.**

70

- Apple Pay: To finish transactions made on this Mac with Apple Pay, use **Touch ID.**
- Apple Books, iTunes Store, and App Store: To finish purchases you make on this Mac from the Apple online stores, use **Touch ID.**
- Password autofill: When utilizing Safari and other programs, Touch ID may be used to automatically fill in usernames, passwords, and credit card information when prompted.
- Quick user switching: On this Mac, utilize **Touch ID to quickly switch between user accounts.**

Rename or delete fingerprints

- Select System Settings from the Apple menu on your Mac, and then select Touch ID & Password on the sidebar. (You might have to scroll below.)
- Take one of the following actions:
  - Rename a fingerprint: To rename a fingerprint, select **the text beneath it and type a new name.**
  - Delete a fingerprint: To remove a fingerprint, select **it, type in your password, select Unlock,** and finally select **Delete.**

Use Touch ID to unlock your Mac, login, or switch users

You must have already entered your password to log into your Mac to use Touch ID for these actions.
- Unlock your Mac and certain password-protected items: Simply press and hold Touch ID when prompted to wake your Mac from sleep or open a password-protected item.
- Open the login window and log in: Put your finger on Touch ID after clicking your name in the login window.
- Touch ID unlocks user accounts only those that have passwords. Touch ID is not available to guests or users that are sharing only.
- To switch users, click the menu bar's rapid user switching option, select a new user, and then press your finger to Touch ID. You must have configured quick user switching and the user you want to switch to must have already logged in to the Mac with a password to use Touch ID to switch to that user.

Use Touch ID to purchase items

- Enter your password to log onto your Mac.
- Buy products from one of the online Apple stores or with Apple Pay.
- When prompted, place your finger on Touch ID.

Print documents

To choose a printer and customize print settings that affect how a document or image appears on paper, use the Print dialog box on your Mac.

- On your Mac, select **File**

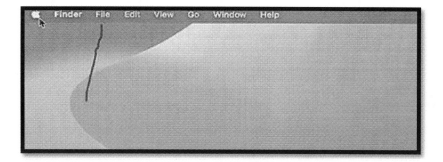

- **Print or hit Command-P** when you have an open document.

A preview of your printed document appears when the Print dialog box opens.

Note: Based on your printer and the application you're running, you may see various options in the Print dialog. Click **Help** in the navigation bar to access the app's documentation if the instructions below don't match what you're seeing.

- Click **Print** to finish if all the options in the Print dialog are correct. If not, move on to step 3.
- Select any of the standard print settings listed below to modify the printing options:

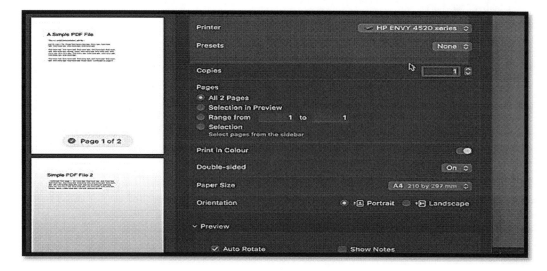

- Printer: Select the printer that you wish to utilize. You can add a printer if one isn't already available.
- Select a preset, which is a collection of print parameters, to use with your document on the printer. Most of the time, you can use the default settings, but you can also select a set of saved settings from an earlier print job.
- **Copies**: Indicate how many copies you would like. Click **Paper Handling,** then choose "**Collate Sheets**" if you want to print every page of a document before the next copy prints.
- **Print Range**: Indicate the number of pages you wish to print. Printing an entire page or a selection of pages is an option. For instance, pages 6 through 9 of a document with 10 pages can be printed. Alternatively, you can use the Selection button to print a subset of the range's pages. To choose the page to print, click its label in the Preview sidebar. Your pick of pages need not be in a straight line. For instance, in a five-page document, you can choose to print pages two and four.
- **Print in Color**: If your printer supports it, choose to print in color. When this option is disabled, documents are printed in black and white.
- **Double-Sided**: If your printer is capable of printing on both sides of paper, select On from the Double-Sided pop-up option. This is also known as duplexing or two-sided printing. To arrange the document to print ready for binding at the top of the page, select **On (Short Edge).**
- Select the paper size that works best for your document. For instance, if the printer is filled with 8.5 by 11-inch paper, select **US Letter.**
- **Orientation**: To change from portrait to landscape orientation, click the icons. Your document's modification can be seen on the preview pages in the sidebar.
- **Scaling:** To fit the printed image on the paper, choose a percentage of scaling. The sidebar of the preview pages now shows the modification.

- Select **Print.**

Keyboard shortcuts

Keyboard shortcuts are combinations of keystrokes that you can use to speed up job completion on your Mac. Keyboard shortcuts involve simultaneously pressing one or more modifier keys (such as Caps Lock or Control) and the last key. For instance, you can hit the Command and N keys to select **File > New Window** instead of dragging the pointer to the menu bar. Keyboard shortcuts can be modified or turned off to make them easier to use. Note: Based on the language and keyboard layout you're using on your Mac, keyboard shortcuts in programs may change. To find the appropriate shortcuts, check the app menus in the menu bar if the ones listed below don't function as you expected. An input source, or your present keyboard layout, can also be viewed with the Keyboard Viewer.

Performing tasks using keyboard shortcuts

Press the last key of the shortcut after holding down one or more modifier keys (such as Caps Lock, Command, or Control). For instance, press and hold the **Command and V keys simultaneously, then release both keys to paste copied text using the Command-V keyboard shortcut.**

Customize keyboard shortcuts

Certain keyboard shortcuts can be altered by swapping out the key combinations.
- To get Keyboard Shortcuts on your Mac, navigate to the **Apple menu > System Settings, and select Keyboard from the sidebar (you might have to scroll down).**
- Choose a category, such as Spotlight or Mission Control, from the list on the left. By selecting the App Shortcuts category on the left, you can also alter the keyboard shortcuts for particular programs.
- Choose the checkbox next to the shortcut you wish to modify from the list on the right.
- To switch to a new key combination, double-click **the one you're using and press it. Every kind of key (like a letter key) can only be used once in a key combination.**
- To activate the new keyboard shortcut, close and reopen any open apps. Your new keyboard shortcut won't function if you use one that is already assigned to another command or application. Either you or the other shortcut has to be changed.

To restore the original key combinations for all shortcuts, navigate to the Keyboard settings, select Keyboard Shortcuts, and then select **Restore Defaults located in the lower-left corner.**

Disable a keyboard shortcut

Keyboard shortcuts for macOS and apps might occasionally conflict. You can turn off the macOS keyboard shortcut if this occurs.
- To get Keyboard Shortcuts on your Mac, navigate to the **Apple menu > System Settings, and select Keyboard from the sidebar (you might have to scroll down).**
- Choose a category, such as Spotlight or Mission Control, from the list on the left.
- To disable a shortcut, deselect the checkbox next to it in the list on the right.

Activity

- Connect my MacBook to a Wi-Fi network?
- What steps do I follow to browse the web securely on my MacBook?

- Preview a file without opening it in an application
- Adjust the display brightness on my MacBook
- Modify the volume on my MacBook
- Set up and use Touch ID on my MacBook
- Enable or disable automatic brightness adjustment on my MacBook
- Mute or unmute the sound on my MacBook
- What are the security benefits of using Touch ID?

CHAPTER 6

BEYOND THE BASICS

Set up a focus to stay on task

Use Focus to keep yourself focused and reduce outside distractions. With a Focus, you may choose to accept only specific alerts, such as those from coworkers on an essential project, or stop and silence all notifications. To let contacts know that you're busy, you can also mention that you've turned off notifications.

Add or remove a Focus

- Select **System Settings from the Apple menu** on your Mac, and then click **Focus** in the sidebar. (You might have to scroll below.)
- **On the right, carry out any of the following:**
  - To add a pre-existing focus, click **Add Focus** and select a focus type, like Work or Gaming.
  - To create a personalized focus, select **Add Focus** and then Custom. Click **OK** after choosing a color and icon and entering a name. You could, for instance, establish a Study Focus. Ten can be created at a time.
  - To switch to a different custom focus, click on it from the list. To modify the Focus's name, color, or icon, click **the icon.**
  - To eliminate a focus, select it from the list and then select **Delete Focus** from the menu at the bottom of the window.

Choose which notifications to allow

When a Focus is active, you may choose which notifications appear—notifications from specific individuals or applications, time-sensitive notifications, or notifications for incoming calls made on your Mac.
Note: Time-sensitive notifications are available in certain apps, like Calendar. Make sure you accept these notifications by choosing to accept them.

- Select **System Settings** from the Apple menu on your Mac, then click **Focus** in the sidebar. (You might have to scroll below.)
- Select a **Focus by clicking on it.**
- **Navigate to Allow Notifications, select Allowed People, and then do any of the following actions by clicking Done;**

- Allow notifications from certain people: Select **Allow Some People** from the option that appears when you click **the notification pop-up**. Select one or more contacts after clicking the **Add People button**. You may, for instance, choose to play multiplayer games with your buddies when choosing the Gaming Focus. Move the pointer over the person you want to remove from the list, then click the **Remove button**.
- **Silence notifications from certain people:** Select **Silence Some People from the option that appears when you click the Notifications pop-up**. Select one or more contacts after clicking the **Add People button**. Drag the pointer over the person you want to remove from the list, and then hit the **Remove button**.
- **Allow notifications for phone calls:** Select an option by clicking the pop-up menu that appears next to "**Allow calls from**." Notifications for calls can come in from everyone, from persons you're allowed to talk to only, from people in your Contacts list, or from people you've added to your Favorites on your iPhone.
- **Allow notifications for repeated phone calls**: To get notifications from anybody who calls twice or more in three minutes, turn on "Allow repeated calls."
- Navigate to Allow Notifications, select **Allowed Apps, and then do any of the following actions by clicking Done.**
  - Select "**Allow Some Apps**" from the Notifications pop-up option to enable notifications from specific apps. After choosing one or more apps, click the Add button. You may, for instance, limit alerts from the apps you use to work-related apps while using the Work Focus. Drag the pointer over the app and select the **Remove button to remove it from the list.**
  - Turn off alerts from certain apps: Select **Silence Some Apps** from the Notifications pop-up option after clicking it. After choosing one or more apps, click the **Add button**. Drag the pointer over the app and select the **Remove button to remove it from the list.**
  - Permit to get alerts about chores or situations that need your urgent attention: Set "Time-sensitive notifications" to on. (Be sure to check the Notifications settings and enable apps to send these notifications as well.)

By default, the Gaming Focus is configured to activate anytime your Mac is connected to a game controller. Make sure to choose individuals or applications to get alerts when the Gaming Focus is activated.

Schedule a Focus to turn on or off instantly

A Focus can be programmed to go on or off automatically at specific times when you arrive at or depart from specific locations, or when you launch or exit specific apps.

- Select **System Settings** from the Apple menu on your Mac, and then click **Focus** in the sidebar. (You might have to scroll below.)
- Select a **Focus by clicking on it.**
- Click **Add Schedule under Set a Schedule**, then choose one of the following actions:
  - Create a timetable by clicking Time, choosing the days of the week that you would like the schedule to run on, and entering the start and end times. Then click Done. Click it once more, adjust the settings, and then click **Done** to modify a time-based schedule. Click **the time-based schedule,** select **Schedule** at the top of the window, and click **Done** to temporarily cease using it.
  - Establish a schedule based on location: After selecting a location and typing a place name into the search area, click **Location again and click Done.** When you set up a Focus to activate depending on the place you are, the Focus activates upon arrival and deactivates upon departure. Click the **location-based schedule, select Automation from the menu at the top of the window, and then click Done to put it on hold**. To use a location, you must have Location Services activated in Privacy settings.
  - Establish an app-based timetable: Click **App**, type the name of an app into the Search bar, pick an app, and click **Done**. When you program a Focus to activate in response to an app, the Focus activates when opening the app and deactivates upon closing it or transitioning to another app. Click the app-based schedule, choose **Automation** from the menu at the top of the window, and then click **Done** to put it on hold.

Customize app behavior

To alter the behavior of Calendar, Mail, Messages, or Safari when a Focus is enabled, add a Focus filter. For instance, when in the Work Focus, select which **Tab Groups to show in Safari**, or conceal your work calendar when in the Personal Focus.

- Select **System Settings from the Apple menu on your Mac**, and then click Focus in the sidebar. (You might have to scroll below.)
- Select a **Focus by clicking on it.**
- Select **Add Filter from Focus Filters**, then take one of the following actions:
  - **Create a Calendar Focus filter:** Choose the calendars you wish to view when this Focus is active by clicking Calendar, then click **Add.**

- ○ **Configure Mail's Focus filter**: Click Mail, choose which email accounts to display when this Focus is on, and then click **Add.**
- ○ **Create a Message Focus Filter**: After selecting **Messages** and activating **Filter by People List**, click **Add.**
- ○ Configure Safari with a Focus filter: Select the **Tab Group** you want to view while this Focus is on, click **Choose next to Tab Group in Safari**, choose whether to enable or disable "Open external links in your Focus Tab Group," and then click **Add.**

You can adjust the Focus Filter settings or temporarily disable it after you've put it up.

- Select **System Settings from the Apple menu**, then click **Focus in the sidebar**, select a **Focus**, and finally select the desired Focus Filter. To adjust the Focus Filter's settings or switch it on or off, use the button at the top of the window. When you're done, click **Done.**

To eliminate a Focus Filter,

- Select **System Settings from the Apple menu, click Focus in the sidebar, select the desired Focus Filter, and then select Delete App Filter at the bottom of the window.**

Share your Focus status

You can configure an app to notify contacts that you have hushed your alerts so they won't know which Focus you are using. Even if it's not urgent, they have the option to let you know.

- Click **Focus in the sidebar after selecting System Settings from the Apple menu on your Mac. (You might have to move down.)**
- Opt for "**Focus status.**"
- "Share Focus status" should be enabled.
- You can choose who can share that you have hushed your notifications by turning each Focus on or off below Share From.

Set up Screen Time for yourself

Screen Time provides you with information about how much time you spend using websites and apps. It also gives you tools to manage how much time you spend on any given task. Screen Time affords parents and guardians the same level of oversight and authority over their children. You can use a passcode to prevent settings changes and individually establish age-appropriate limits and restrictions for each child. To find out how much time you spend on your Mac and other devices, turn on Screen Time on your Mac. **You can see reports that display app usage, the number of alerts you receive, and how frequently you use your devices when Screen Time is enabled.**

- Select System Settings from the Apple menu on your Mac, and then select **Screen Time** in the sidebar. (You might have to scroll below.)
- In a Family Sharing group, if you are a parent or guardian, select yourself by clicking the **Family Member pop-up option on the right.**
- To activate app and website activity, select **App & Website Activity and then Turn On.**
- **After selecting the Back button and swiping down, activate any of the following settings:**
  - Transfer between devices: If you would want Screen Time reports to incorporate time spent on additional devices that are connected to the same Apple ID, turn this option on. You can only access this option when logged in with your Apple ID.
  - Enable the "**Lock Screen Time Settings**" option to extend the time after limits expire and make Screen Time settings require a passcode. Note: You are requested to change the family member's administrator account to a regular account if they have one.

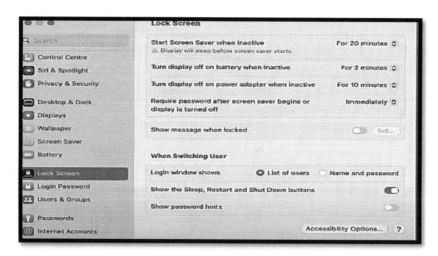

- **In the Screen Time configurations, do any of the following;**
  - Click **Notifications, Pickups, or App & Website Activity to examine your device and app usage.**
  - Create a downtime schedule by clicking **Downtime.**
  - To set time limitations for websites and applications, click **App limitations.**
  - Select the apps that can be used whenever you want by clicking **Always Allowed.**
  - To get notifications when you're holding a smartphone too close, click Screen Distance.

- ○ Select **Communication Limits** and then adjust the limits.
- ○ To check for sensitive photos, click **Communication Safety.**
- ○ To set up content and privacy restrictions, click **Content & Privacy.**

Use Dictation

You can dictate text anyplace you can type it by simply speaking into Dictation. Dictation requests are handled on your device for supported languages on a Mac running Apple silicon; an internet connection is not necessary. Dictated text entered into a search box may be forwarded to the search provider so that the search can be processed. You can also dictate any length of text without having to wait for a timeout. Dictation can be turned off manually or it can shut off on its own after 30 seconds if no voice is detected. Your dictated words are transferred to Apple for processing when you dictate on an Intel-based Mac or in a dialect that doesn't allow on-device dictation. **Note:** Features may differ and dictation may not be available in all languages, countries, or areas. For information on supported on-device processing and dictation languages, visit the macOS Feature Availability webpage. Use Voice Control if you need to dictate text and operate your Mac without a keyboard and trackpad. View Make use of Voice Control prompts. Dictation is not available while Voice Control is used.

Turn on Dictation

- Select **System Settings from the Apple menu on your Mac, and then click Keyboard from the sidebar. (You might have to scroll below.)**

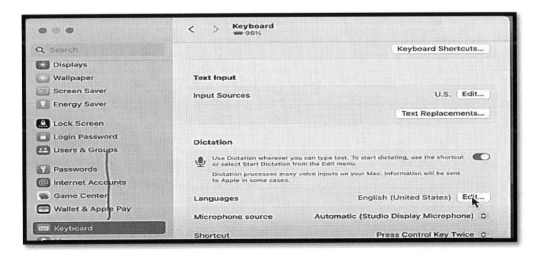

- Navigate to **Dictation** by turning it on on the right. In case a prompt shows up, select **Enable.**
- **When prompted to enhance Siri and Dictation, choose from the following actions:**
  ○ Distribute audio recordings: To permit Apple to record the sound of your Mac Siri and Dictation interactions, click **Share Audio Recordings. An example of stored audio may be reviewed by Apple.**
  ○ Never distribute audio recordings: Select "**Not Now.**"
- If you decide later on to share or not share audio recordings, go to System Settings from the Apple menu, then select **Privacy & Security from the sidebar. (You might have to scroll below.)** Navigate to **Analytics & Improvements on the right, and then select the option to Enable or Disable Siri & Dictation.** Note: You are free to remove the audio interactions at any time. They are under six months old and are linked to a random identifier.
- You can choose a language and dialect to dictate by clicking the **Edit button** next to Languages. (Deselect a language to delete it.)

Dictate Text

- Position the insertion point where you would like the dictated text to appear in a Mac app.
- If the microphone key is present in the function key row, press it. Alternatively, you can select **Edit**

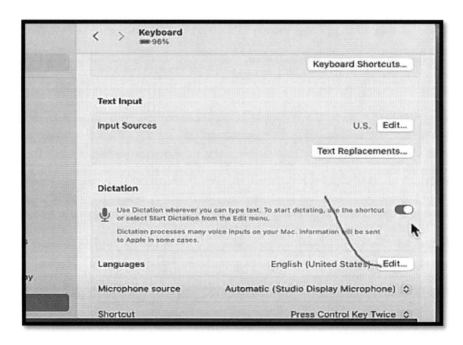

> Start Dictation or utilize the Dictation keyboard shortcut. Note: To begin Dictation, press and release the Microphone key. To activate Siri, press and hold the Microphone key (Siri needs to be enabled).

- Dictate your text when the microphone symbol shows up above or below a highlighted cursor, or when you hear the alert tone on your Mac indicating that it's ready for dictation. You don't have to stop dictating if you're using a Mac with Apple hardware to enter text while dictating. As you type, the microphone symbol vanishes; it resurfaces when you finish typing, allowing you to continue dictating.
- You can use any of the following to add a punctuation mark or an emoji, or to carry out basic formatting tasks:
  - Emoji names, such as "heart emoji" or "car emoji," should be said.
  - Declare the punctuation mark's name, for example, "exclamation mark."
  - Say "new line," which is the same as hitting the Return key once, or "new paragraph," which is the same as hitting the Return key twice. When you finish dictating, a new paragraph or line appears.

Note: As you dictate, Dictation automatically inserts question marks, commas, and periods in the languages it supports. Click Keyboard in the sidebar after selecting Apple menu > System Settings to disable this feature. (You might have to scroll below.) After selecting Dictation on the right, disable Auto-punctuation.

- Click the language adjacent to the microphone or press the Globe key, and then select the language you wish to use, if you have Dictation set up for many languages and want to switch between them while you dictate.

- Once finished, hit the **Escape key or the Dictation keyboard shortcut.** After 30 seconds without any identified speech, the dictation automatically ends.

Unclear text is highlighted in blue. For instance, if you type in the word "flower," you can receive the result "flour." In that scenario, click the highlighted word and choose a different option. The right text can also be dictated or typed.

Change the microphone used for Dictation

The device that your Mac is now utilizing to listen for Dictation is displayed by the microphone source in the Keyboard settings.

- Select **System Settings** from the Apple menu on your Mac, then click Keyboard from the sidebar. (You might have to scroll below.)
- Navigate to the **Dictation section on the right,** and select the **microphone you wish to use for Dictation** by clicking the pop-up menu next to "Microphone source."

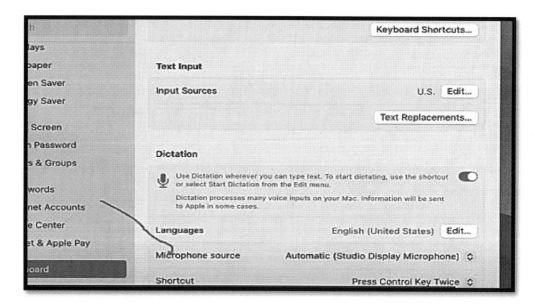

Your Mac responds to the gadget you use most frequently for Dictation if you select Automatic.

Turn off Dictation

- Select **System Settings** from the Apple menu on your Mac, and then click Keyboard from the sidebar. (You might have to scroll below.)
- Navigate to **Dictation** by turning it off on the right.

Send emails

Emails can be sent, scheduled to be sent later, and saved as drafts. You must add at least one email account to the Mail app before you may send an email.

Send an email

- Select the **New Message button** located in the Mail toolbar of the Mail software on your Mac.

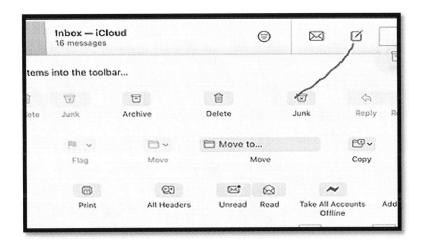

- Enter the email address you wish to send the message to in the To area. To preserve the privacy of your recipients, you can also conceal everyone's email address when sending emails to a group of addresses using your Contacts app.
- Fill in the **Subject field with the subject of your email.**

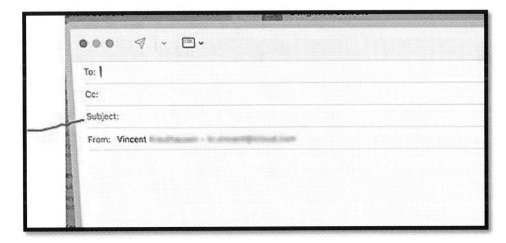

- Type your message in the Message field (below the subject). Emails can have their text formatted, and attachments containing images and other information can be sent.
- Press the "Send" button.

Save a draft

- Make sure you are in the message you wish to save in the Mac Mail program.
- Select **File > Save**. Another option is to click on **Save in the resulting dialog box after closing the message window.**
- You can access your draft from the Favorites bar or the Mail sidebar, or you can find it in the Drafts inbox.

Schedule an email

Choose from the following actions in the Mac Mail app:
- Plan a correspondence email: Select a time by clicking the pop-up menu that appears next to the Send button, or select **Send Later to specify a date and time.**

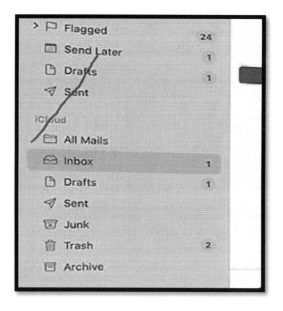

The email shows up in the Mail sidebar's Send Later mailbox.
- Modify the email's planned time: To edit the email, double-click it **in the Send Later mailbox** and select **Edit from the upper-right corner.**
- Stop an email that is scheduled to be sent: Click the **Delete button after selecting the email in the Send Later mailbox.**

Send text messages

Send an infinite number of messages to anyone logged into iMessage on an Apple device with an Apple ID by using iMessage, a secure messaging service. iMessage-sent messages show up as blue text bubbles. You can use your Mac to send SMS messages to any mobile phone, provided that your iPhone is running iOS 8.1 or later. SMS messages show up as green text bubbles.

Get messages on your Mac using iMessage

- Insert your Apple ID and password in the Messages program on your Mac, and then select **Sign In.**

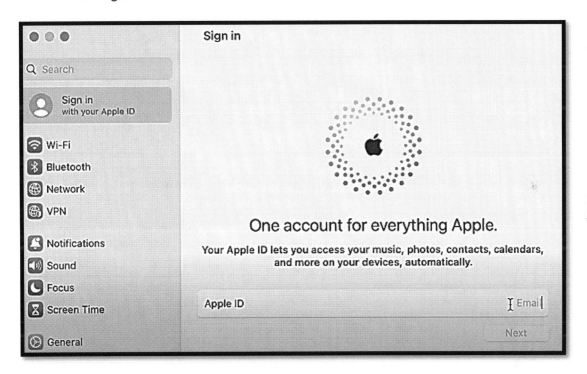

- Ensure that you log in to all of your devices using the same Apple ID.
- Visit the Apple ID account website if you need to set up an Apple ID or if you've forgotten your password.
- Click any of the following choices after choosing **Messages > Settings**

- Clicking iMessage

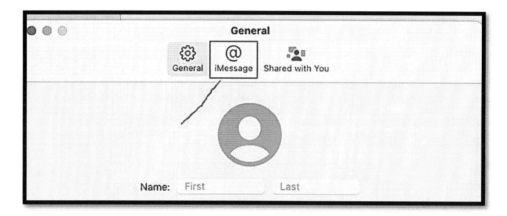

- And then clicking Settings:

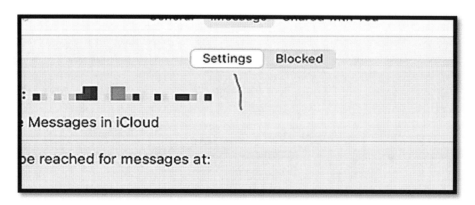

○ To store your messages in iCloud, turn on the "**Enable Messages in iCloud**" option.

View Configure iCloud Messages on every device you own. Note: The iCloud settings allow you to enable or disable Messages in iCloud.

○ Messages can be directed to you at: Decide which phone numbers or email addresses you want people to use to contact you.
○ Transmit read receipts: Tick this box to let others who send you messages know when you've responded. Additionally, read receipts for a particular chat can be sent.
○ Establish new conversations select the phone number or email address you wish to use to initiate new discussions. The ability to select multiple email addresses or phone numbers beneath "You can be reached for messages at" is limited to those who possess these details. It should be noted that when you send a message, this is what other people see. Conversations with other people display your phone number, for instance, if you have it selected.

Send a message on Mac

Once you've configured Messages on your Mac, you may send messages with text, images, animation effects, and more to an individual, a group of individuals, or an organization.
One can express themselves in a variety of ways:
- Tapbacks
- Photos and videos
- Stickers and images
- Audio messages

- Message effects
- To begin a new message in the Messages program on your Mac, select the **Compose button (or use the Touch Bar).**

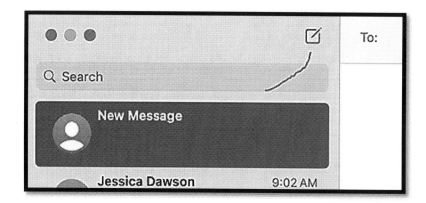

- In the designated To field, provide the recipient's name, email address, or phone number. Messages propose addresses as you type, either from contacts in your Contacts app or from people you've messaged before. In addition, you have the option to click the **Add button to the right of the To area.** After selecting a contact from the list, click t**he phone number or email address.** Note: An hourglass icon will show up next to the names of the persons you are unable to message if you are only able to send and receive messages with specific individuals.
- In the space provided at the window's bottom, type your message. If accessible, you can use the typing suggestions.
- On your keyboard, press **Return to send the message.**

Make a FaceTime video call

With an Apple device that satisfies these requirements, users can see and converse with each other during FaceTime video chats. The Wi-Fi connection on your Mac is used for FaceTime video conversations.
- Click **New FaceTime in the Mac FaceTime app.**
- Enter the person you wish to call, phone number, or email address in the New FaceTime window. You might have to hit Return. You can enter the person's name or choose them from Suggested if they are already in your Contacts. Additionally, contacts from the New FaceTime window can be added.

- Choose **FaceTime**, or you can also choose to make use of the Touch Bar.

Answer FaceTime video call

Even when FaceTime is closed, you can still take calls provided you're logged in and have FaceTime enabled. View the requirements for FaceTime video and audio calls. **When a notification shows in the upper-right corner of the screen on your Mac, choose one of the following actions:**

- Click **Accept** to answer an incoming call.
- Receive a video call just like any other call: Select Answer as Audio after clicking the down arrow next to Accept. The camera turns off automatically when you're on a phone call or audio call.
- Take a call, and then end the one you're on: Select "**End & Accept.**"
- Decline a call: Select Decline. To send a text message or set a reminder, you may additionally select the down arrow next to **Decline.**

Decline a FaceTime video call

Even when FaceTime is closed, you can reject calls provided you are logged in and have FaceTime enabled.

When a notification shows in the upper-right corner of the screen on your Mac, choose one of the following actions:

- **Refuse a call:** Select **Decline**. The person calling notices that you're not in the office.
- **Reject a call and use iMessage to deliver a message:** Select **Reply** with reply from the drop-down menu by clicking the arrow next to Decline, enters your reply, and hit Send. The caller and you both need to be logged into iMessage.
- **Turn down a call and make a note to call back later:** To set the time for when you wish to get a reminder, select the down arrow beside the Decline. Whenever the time comes, a notification appears on your screen. Select it to see the reminder, and click the link to initiate the call.

End a FaceTime video call

Move the cursor over the call window and select the "**Leave Call**" button (or use the Touch Bar) to end the call.

Edit photos and videos

You can rapidly crop and rotate images, add filters, edit photos, and do much more with the Photos editing tools. You can copy edits to other photographs and duplicate photos to experiment with different settings. You can reverse the edits you made to a photo if you don't like them.

Edit a photo or video

- One of the following actions can be taken in the Mac's Photos app:
  - Double-click the thumbnail of an image or video,

- Then select **Edit from the toolbar.**

- Choose **a thumbnail image or video, and then hit Return.**
- **Get any of the following done;**
  - Select or drag the Zoom **slider to enlarge or reduce the size of a photo.**
  - Make changes: To view the adjustment tools, click **Adjust.**

- Apply filters: To alter the appearance of your picture or video, click the **Filters button.**

- ○ **Trim the picture**: To see the options for cropping a picture or video, click **Crop**.
- ○ **Rotate a picture or video**: To rotate an image counterclockwise, select the Rotate button on the toolbar. Click again and again until you achieve the desired alignment. For a clockwise rotation of the image, option-click the button.
- ○ Enhance a picture or video automatically: To have your picture or video's color and contrast automatically altered, select the Auto Enhance option. Use Command-Z or select Revert to Original to undo the changes.
- • To put an end to editing, choose **Done or tap Return.**

Duplicate a photo

You make copies of photos and videos and work on the copies to create multiple versions of them.
- • Choose the object you wish to duplicate from the Photos app on your Mac.
- • Select **Image > Duplicate 1 Picture (or hit Command-D).** Click **Duplicate** to include the video when duplicating a live photo, or Duplicate as Still Photo to include only the still image.

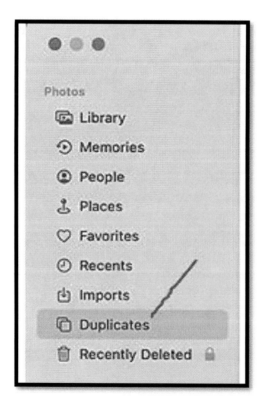

Compare photos or videos before and after editing

You can make a comparison between the altered and original form of an item while editing it.

- Double-click **a picture or video** to open it in the Photos app on your Mac, then **select Edit from the toolbar.**
- Press and hold the **M key or click and hold the Without Adjustments icon** to view the original image. To view the item with revisions, release the icon or the M key.

Copy and paste edits

You can duplicate and paste your edited photos or videos onto other objects when you've finished editing them. Edits can be pasted onto several items at once.
Note: The retouch tool, red-eye tool, crop tool, and third-party extensions do not allow you to copy and paste their settings.

- Double-click **an edited object in the Photos app on your Mac, then select Edit from the toolbar.**
- Select **Image** > **Copy Adjustments.**
- To apply the edits, click **the item you want to change (or Command-click several items).**
- Select **Paste Edits under Image.**

Note however that you can also choose to Control-click an object in the editing view and then select Copy Edits or Paste Edits.

Undo your changes

It's easy to undo edits made to a picture or video. Using the Mac's Photos app, choose one of the following actions:

- Reverse the previous alteration you made: Either hit Command-Z or select **Edit** > **Undo.**
- Restore the initial image and undo all of your changes: Once the image or video has been selected, select **Image** > **Revert to Original.**

Use Live Text to interact with text in a photo

The text that is displayed in a photo can be copied and used using Live Text in Photos. For instance, you may copy and paste words from a roadside sign into an email or text message.

- Launch a photo that displays text in your Mac's Photos program.
- To select the text, move the pointer over it and drag.

- **Take one of the following actions:**
- **Copy the text:** Select what you want to copy by control-clicking on it or by pressing
  - Command-C. After that, you can paste the text into another app or document.
  - **Look up the text's meaning:** Select your choice, then control-click to select Lookup [text].
  - **Translate this text:** Select Translate [text] with a control-click on your selection, and then select a language. Note: Not all languages have translations available, and not all nations or regions may have translations available.
  - **Look up the text online:** Select your pick using a control click, then select [web search engine] for search.
  - **Distribute the text to other people:** Select it with a control click, select Share, and then select the text's sharing option.
  - **Make contact with a phone number:** To make a call, initiate a FaceTime audio or video call, send a message to the number, control-click your selection, or click the down arrow.
  - **Reach out via email:** You can either create an email or add the email address to Contacts by control-clicking your selection or by using the down arrow.
  - **Visit this website:** To view the information on the website, control-click your selection, clicks the down arrow, and then opens the link in your internet browser or use Quick Look.

Start a Quick Note

You can add links and scribble thoughts in Quick Note regardless of anything else you're working on on your Mac. You can quickly select and add data from other apps to your Quick Note because it remains visible on the screen while it is open.

Start a Quick Note

- Use the shortcut by holding down the Fn or Globe key and then pressing **Q on the keyboard.**
- To utilize hot corners, move the pointer to the **Quick Notes default hot corner in the bottom-right corner of the screen, then click the note that displays.** Employ hot corners to adjust or disable the hot corner.

- Utilize Safari
- Select the red Close button located in the upper left corner of a Quick Note to end it. Use any of the aforementioned methods to open the Quick Note once more.

To ensure that a fresh Quick Note is always opened instead of the old one being opened, click **Notes > Settings** and uncheck the box next to "Always resume to last Quick Note."

Add Safari links to a Quick Note

- Launch the webpage you want to connect to in the Mac's Safari program.
- Select **New Quick Note or Add to Quick Note after clicking the Share button**. A reminder of your previous notes appears as a thumbnail of the Quick Note in the corner of the screen when you navigate back to the webpage with the related material.

Links to other apps and websites can also be added to Notes.

Add content from Safari to a Quick Note

On a webpage, you can select text and add it straight to a Quick Note.

- Open a webpage in the Safari program on your Mac, and then pick the text you wish to add to a Quick Note.
- Select **New Quick Note or Add to Quick Note by controlling-clicking the text.** The text in Safari is highlighted, and a link appears in the Quick Note. The text remains highlighted even after you return to the webpage.

Remove the Safari link from the Quick Note to get rid of the highlights.

Get Directions

Directions for driving, walking, using public transit, and cycling are available. You can add more stops to your route when driving.

For easy access while on the road, you may also email the directions to your iPhone, iPad, or Apple Watch.

Note: Not all nations or areas have directions for numerous stops.

- Choose from the following actions in the **Mac's Maps app**:
    - After selecting **the Directions button** from the toolbar, input the beginning and destination locations.
    - After selecting your location—such as a landmark or pin on a map—click the **Directions button** on the place card. You can enter a different starting point, but Maps utilizes the one that is now displayed. To change the positions of your beginning and conclusion, you can also drag the **Reorder button next to the place.**
- Select **the option that says Drive, Walk, Transit, or Cycle.**
- To view the list of directions, click **the Trip Details icon adjacent to a route.** When driving, some possible directions are:
    - Route planning for electric vehicles: Look for charging stations along the way and monitor your vehicle's current charge (if it fits).
    - Congestion zones: These areas serve to alleviate traffic in densely populated parts of large cities such as Singapore, London, and Paris. When these zones are in effect, you can find a route around them.
    - License plate restrictions: Depending on your eligibility, you can obtain a route through or around a restricted area in Chinese cities that restricts entry to populated areas. In some cities, directions are accessible for those who choose to bike.
- **Get any of the following done;**
    - Focus on a single step: In the list of instructions, click **the step.**
    - Select when you want to depart or arrive: Click **Plan** to select when you want to leave or arrive if you're driving or using public transit.
    - Select the **Trip Details button** once more to close the directions list.

Activity

- Set Screen Time limits for specific apps.
- Dictate text into documents or emails?
- Create a new email and set up signatures.
- What's the difference between iMessage and Text Edit?
- Initiate a FaceTime call with a friend?
- Use Live Text to extract phone numbers from photos.
- Take screenshots or screen recordings?

CHAPTER 7
FILES AND FOLDERS

Create and work with documents

You can generate reports, essays, spreadsheets, financial charts, presentations, slideshows, and many other things with macOS tools like Pages and TextEdit or Mac App Store apps.

Create documents

- Open a document creation application on your Mac. To create a plain text, rich text, or HTML document, for instance, launch **TextEdit.**
- Either select **File**

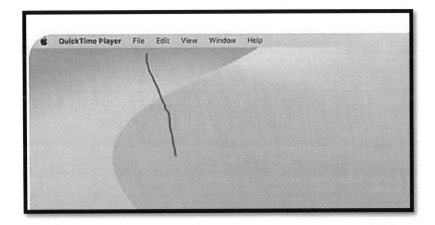

- **New or click New Document** in the Open dialog box. This Apple software, which may be used to make reports, spreadsheets, presentations, and more, is included with a lot of Mac computers:
  - **Pages**: Produce flyers, posters, reports, letters, and more. Pages have a ton of templates that make it simple to create documents with style.
  - **Numbers**: To arrange and display your data, make spreadsheets. Take a template and make any changes you want to it, such as adding charts, photos, formulas, and more.
  - **Keynote**: Use graphics, media, charts, slide animations, and other elements to create captivating presentations.

You can get Pages, Numbers, and Keynote from the App Store if you don't already have them on your Mac. Additionally, you can get them on iCloud.com and through the App Store for your iOS and iPadOS devices.

Format documents

On your Mac, you can format and manipulate text in documents in several ways:
- In a document, select **Format > Show Fonts, Format > Font > Show Fonts**, or **Format > Style** to change the fonts and styles.
- To alter a document's color scheme, select **Format > Show Colors or Format > Font > Show Colors**.
- Enter a variety of character kinds, including diacritical and accented characters.
- Verify your spelling: Most apps check your spelling as you type, immediately correcting any errors. You have additional options or can disable these features.
- Verify definitions by selecting the desired text in a document, **Control-clicking it, and selecting Look Up**.
- To translate text, pick the text in the document, Control-click it, and select Translate.

Save documents

Your Mac's many programs automatically store your documents as you work. A document can be saved at any moment.
- Save a document: In a document, select **File > Save, type a name, and select a location (click the down arrow button to reveal more options)**, and then click **Save**.

- You can annotate your document with tags to make it more easily located once you save it. Your document might be able to be saved in iCloud Drive, making it accessible from computers as well as iOS and iPadOS devices that have iCloud Drive set up.
- Save a file under a different name: Select **File > Save As in a document,** then type a new name. Press and hold the Option key to bring up the File menu once more if Save As isn't visible.
- Save a file as a duplicate: Select **File > Duplicate or File > Save As** when working on a document.

Additionally, you can save a document as a PDF and merge several files into one.

Open documents

Double-clicking the desktop icon of a document is the fastest way to open it on a Mac. **Alternatively, you can open a document on your Mac in case its icon isn't visible on the desktop:**

- Select Spotlight from the menu bar, type the name of a document into the search field, and then double-click the document that appears in the results.
- Select the document from the **Apple menu > Recent Items** if you have worked on it recently.
- Launch the app that is linked with the document, select it from the Open dialog box (if it appears), or select **File > Open.** To view documents you've recently used, select **File > Open Recent in certain programs.**
- In the Dock, click the Finder icon. Double-click the document's name or icon after selecting it from the Finder sidebar by clicking **Recents, iCloud Drive, Documents, or the folder containing it.**

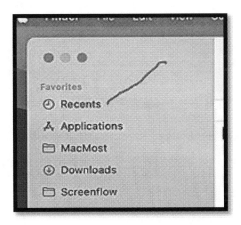

On a Mac, files made with Microsoft Office can be opened. To access Microsoft Word documents, Excel spreadsheets, and PowerPoint presentations, use the Pages app, Numbers app, and Keynote app, respectively. You can get Pages, Numbers, and Keynote from the App Store if you don't already have them on your Mac.

Mark up files

With Markup on your Mac, you can annotate, sign, and sketch on PDF documents and photos as well as resize and rotate them. With Continuity Markup, you can annotate a file on your iPhone or iPad—even with an Apple Pencil on the iPad—and see the changes on your Mac instantly if your device is closed. Your devices must meet system requirements and have Wi-Fi and Bluetooth® turned on to activate Continuity features.

- Click the **Markup tool in Quick Look on your Mac**. Or select Markup while utilizing Quick Actions. Other programs that support markup include Mail, Notes, TextEdit, and Photos.
- On your Mac, mark up an image or a PDF document using the tools described below. The tools offered change based on the kind of file. You can annotate a file using Continuity Markup on your iPhone or iPad if it's close by. Click **Revert to undo any changes you don't like, then try again.**

Combine files into a PDF

You may easily merge several files into a PDF directly from a Finder window or your desktop.

- To launch a Finder window on your Mac, select the **Finder icon in the Dock.**
- Choose the files that you wish to merge into a PDF. You also have the option of choosing the files from your desktop. Keep in mind that the files show up in the PDF in the same sequence that you choose.

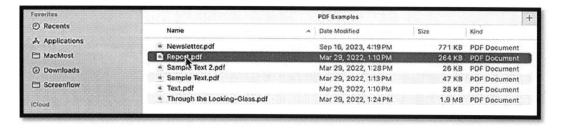

- Select the files with a control-click, then select **Quick Actions > Create PDF**. A file with a name resembling the first file you chose is automatically created.

Additionally, you can utilize the Create PDF icon in the Preview pane of a Finder window after selecting the files in the Finder. Select **View** > **Show Preview** if the Preview pane isn't shown on the right.

Organize files on your desktop

Turn on desktop stacks

- Click the desktop and select **View** > **Use Stacks** on your Mac

- Or hit Control-Command-0. Alternatively, you can Control-click the desktop and select Use Stacks.

Browse files in a desktop stack

Using two fingers on the trackpad or one finger on a Magic Mouse, swipe left or right on the stack on your Mac.

Change how desktop stacks are grouped

Stacks can be categorized by Finder tags, date (like the last time a file was generated or accessed), or kind (like photos or PDFs).

- Click the desktop, select **View** > **Group Stacks By,** and then select an option on your Mac. Alternatively, Control-click the desktop, selects Group Stacks By, and then picks a preference.

Change the appearance of desktop stacks

You can adjust the icon sizes, label positions, and spacing, as well as display other information (such as the number of files in a stack).

- Click the desktop, select **View > Show View Options**, and then make any necessary changes. Alternatively, Control-click **the desktop**, select **Show View Options, and then modify the settings.**

Organize files with folders

On your Mac, everything is arranged into folders, including documents, images, audio, programs, and more. You may make new folders while you work, add apps, and create documents to help you stay organized.

Create a folder

- To create a folder on your Mac, select the Finder icon in the Dock to launch a Finder window and then go to the desired location. If you would prefer to create the folder on the desktop, you may also click the desktop.
- Press **Shift-Command-N, or select File > New Folder.**

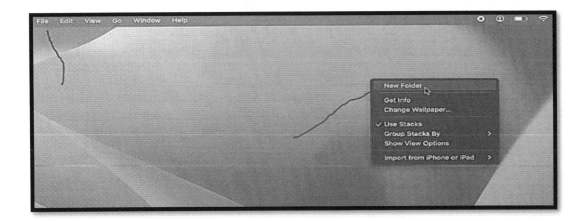

You are unable to make a folder in the current location if the New Folder command is darkened.

- After giving the folder a name, hit **Return**.

Move items into folders

To launch a Finder window on your Mac, select the Finder icon in the Dock.
Take one of the following actions:

- Drag an object into a folder to place it there.
- Place many objects inside a folder: After choosing an item, drag it into the folder. The chosen things all go into the folder.
- Place the contents of a window in a folder: Once an icon appears, move the pointer directly to the left of the window title and drag it to the folder. When you drag the pointer into the title box, you can press and hold **the Shift key** to make the icon appear right away. Alternatively, you can drag the window title from the start to the folder without having to wait for the icon to show up.
- Store something in its original place and place a duplicate inside a folder: After choosing the object, hold down the **Option key** and drag it into the folder.
- Save anything in the original spot and create a new folder alias for it: To create the alias, press and hold the **Option and Command keys while dragging the object into the folder.**
- Create a duplicate of something in the same folder: After selecting the item, hit Command-D or select **File > Duplicate**.
- Transfer files to another disk: Files can be dragged to the disk.
- Transfer files to another disk: Holding down the Command key will allow you to drag the files to the drive.

Move two folders with the same name

You can combine two folders with the same name that are located in different places into one larger folder.

- To move a folder with the same name to a different place on your Mac first hit and hold the Option key. Click **Merge in the popup that pops up.**
- Only when there are items in one of the folders that are not in the other does the Merge option show up. The only choices are Stop or Replace if the directories include multiple versions of files with the same name.

Tag files and folders

To make files and folders easier to locate, you can tag them. Whether you store your files and folders in iCloud or on your Mac, Tags are compatible with all of them.

Tag files and folders

Every document or folder can have many tags added to it.
Try any of these suggestions on your Mac:

- Using the pointer to the right of the document title, select the down arrow, click in the **Tags field and either type a new tag or select one from the list to tag an open file.**
- When you save a new file, tag it: Select **File > Save**. Select in the **Tags field of the Save dialog box, type a new tag, or select one from the list.**
- Tag a file in the Finder or on the desktop: After choosing the item, the File menu will appear. Moreover, you can Control-click the object. Select a color above Tags (as you move the cursor over the color, the tag name replaces Tags); alternatively, click **Tags to select more tags or to add a new tag**. You can also pick the item in a Finder window, click the **Tags button, type a new tag**, or select **one from the list.**

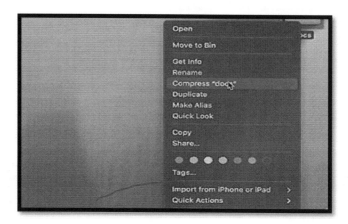

Find items you tagged

To launch a Finder window on your Mac, select the Finder icon in the Dock.

Take one of the following actions:

- Look for a tag: Type the name or color of the tag into the search bar, then choose the tag from the list of options.

- Choose a tag from the sidebar: Click the **tag in the Finder sidebar to view everything that has that tag.**
- To modify the tags displayed in the sidebar, pick **Finder > Settings, click Tags, and then choose which tags to display.**
- Sort items using a tag: Select **Tags after clicking the Group button.**
- Sort the objects using a tag: Select **View > Show View Options in any view**, then tap the **Sort By pop-up box and select Tags.** To see the Tags column in List view, move the cursor over it and click it after selecting the Tags checkbox.

Remove tags

Try one of the following on your Mac:

- Take off the tags from a product: Control-click **the object on the desktop or in a Finder window, and select Tags. Click Delete after selecting the tags you wish to get rid of.**

- Take tags off of your Mac: Select **Finder > Settings from the Finder menu**, then select **Tags**. Click the **Remove button** after selecting the tags you wish to remove.

Edit tags

- Select **Finder > Settings** from within the Mac Finder, and then click Tags.

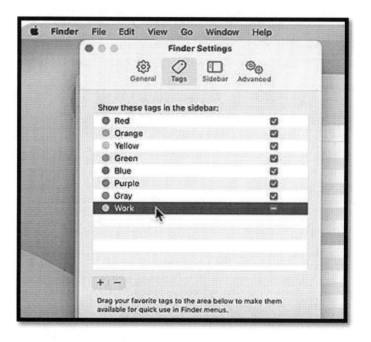

- Take one of the following actions:
  - Notice a tag in the sidebar of Finder: Next to the tag, select the **blue checkbox.**
  - To alter the color of a tag, click **on the color adjacent to it and select a different one.**
  - To change the name of a tag, click it, click **its name, and then type a new name.**
  - Select the **Add button to create a new tag.**
  - Eliminate a tag: After choosing the tag, press the **Remove button.**

- Give the shortcut menu a tag: To change a tag, choose it from the list and drag it over the current tag in the window's favorites area. When you Control-click a file, a shortcut menu appears with up to seven tags.
- Eliminate a tag from the menu shortcut: When the "remove" indication appears, drag the tag out of the Favorite Tags box.

Backup files

You may use Time Machine to backup non-macOS installation files from your computer, including documents, music, images, programs, and photographs. Time Machine automatically backs up your Mac and creates hourly, daily, and weekly file backups when it is turned on. Even though your backup disk is not connected, Time Machine preserves local snapshots that you can utilize to retrieve earlier versions of files. These hourly snapshots are made, kept on the same drive as the initial files, and kept there for a maximum of 24 hours, or until the disk needs more space. You can only make local snapshots on drives that use the Apple File System (APFS). It is advised that you back up your files to a destination other than your main disk, such as an external hard drive, a disk on your network, or a Time Capsule, even if Time Machine generates local snapshots on machines running APFS. In this manner, you can restore your whole system to a different Mac if something were to happen to your internal drive or your Mac.

- Turn on the external hard drive after connecting it to your Mac. Important: You can only restore files from a backup that you make on a Mac running macOS 12 or later to a Mac running macOS 11 or later.
- **Get any of the following done;**
    - From the "Time Machine can back up your Mac" window, create a disk: You're prompted to use the disk to back up your Mac if you don't already have one set up for Time Machine. Move your cursor over the resulting dialog box, select Options, and then select **Set Up to utilize this disk with Time Machine as a backup disk. (If you select Close, the disk attaches normally and Time Machine closes.)**
    - In the Time Machine Settings, configure a disk: Select **Open Time Machine Settings** after clicking the Time Machine icon in the navigation bar.
    - Select **Apple menu > System Settings** if the Time Machine symbol isn't visible in the menu bar. To access the Time Machine, select **Control Center** in the sidebar, go down to it, and choose "**Show in Menu Bar**" from the pulldown option.
- Choose **Add Backup Disk or choose the Add button +**. The available choice is based on if you have one or more backup disks that have already been configured.

Restore files

You may simply restore older versions of files or retrieve lost objects if you utilize Time Machine to back up your Mac's contents.

- Open the item's window on your Mac to begin the restoration process. For instance, open the Documents folder to retrieve a file that you unintentionally erased. It is not necessary to open a window if something is missing from the desktop.
- Open Time Machine (located in the Other folder) using Launchpad. While your Mac is connecting to the backup disk, a notice can show up.
- To browse the local backups and snapshots, use the timeline and arrows. A backup that is still processing or validating on the backup drive is indicated by a pulsating light to a semi-dark gray tick mark.
- Click **Restore** after selecting one or more objects you wish to restore (you can restore folders or your entire disk). Restored things go back where they were originally. For instance, if anything was in the Documents folder, it gets put back there.

You can browse older versions of documents in Time Machine with many programs by selecting **File > Revert To > Browse All Versions.** From there, you may locate and restore the desired version. Your documents, pictures, and videos may be safely stored in iCloud with the help of iCloud Drive and iCloud Photos.

Recover files using Time Machine and Spotlight on Mac

If you back up your Mac using Time Machine, you can utilize Spotlight to search Time Machine for deleted or lost files. Note: You may access previous versions of files from within programs like TextEdit and Preview, which allow you to create and save documents.

- Launch the **Finder app on your Mac,** then enter a term or phrase into the search bar in the top-right corner.
- Use the search field to narrow down the results by entering specific search parameters.
- Select **Browse Time Machine** backups after clicking the **Time Machine icon in the navigation bar.** Select **Apple menu > System Settings** if the Time Machine symbol isn't visible in the menu bar. To access the Time Machine, select **Control Center in the sidebar, go down to it, and choose "Show in Menu Bar" from the pulldown option.**
- Navigate through the **Time Machine backups using the timeline and arrows.**
- Click **Restore after selecting one or more objects** you wish to restore (you can restore folders or your whole disk). Restored things go back where they were originally. For instance, if anything was in the Documents folder, it gets put back there.

Activity

- Create a new document in Pages or another program.
- Combine multiple documents (like a Word doc and images) into a single PDF.
- Organize my files with folders on my Macbook.
- Create custom tags for files and folders to make searching easier.
- Back up files to ensure they're safe? (External hard drive, cloud storage, etc.?)

CHAPTER 8

APPS

App Store

Get the most recent updates for your apps by searching the App Store for apps to download.

- **Find the perfect app**: Are you certain of what you want? In the search field, type the name of the program and hit **Return**. When you download an app from the App Store, Launchpad opens it automatically. Alternatively, you can go through the results of a sidebar tab selection such as Create, Work, or Play to discover new apps.

- **All you need is an Apple ID**: Sign in with your Apple ID by clicking Sign In at the bottom of the App Store sidebar to download free apps. Click Sign In, then select **Create Apple ID if you don't already have one.** To retrieve your password if you have an Apple ID but can't remember it, click "**Forgot Apple ID or password?**" To purchase fee-based apps, you must also create an account and provide payment details.

- **Use iPhone and iPad apps on your Mac**: You can use a lot of iPhone and iPad apps on your MacBook Air. On your Mac, any accessible apps that you earlier bought for your iPad or iPhone are displayed. Check if an app is available on Mac by searching for it in the App Store.

- **Game on**: To monitor your achievement progress, see games you can play, games that are popular with your Game Center friends learn how to subscribe to Apple Arcade, and more, click the Arcade tab. Even with a gaming controller, games you obtain from the App Store are always accessible because they automatically show up in Launchpad's Games folder.

- **Game Mode**: Game Mode automatically reduces background task utilization by giving games the highest priority on your Mac's CPU and GPU when you're playing them. For tangible responsiveness, it also significantly lowers latency when using wireless devices like AirPods and your preferred controllers.

- **Save your game action**: On third-party game controllers that are compatible, you can record and share up to a 15-second gameplay video clip. This allows you to evaluate your game strategy or capture special gaming moments.

- **Invite your friends to play**: It's simple to invite your recent Messages pals and groups to play games that support Game Center with the new multiplayer friend picker. View the friend request inbox to view incoming requests and invitations.

- **Get the latest app updates**: There are updates accessible if the App Store symbol in the Dock has a badge on it. To access the App Store, click the icon, and then select Updates from the sidebar.

Books

You can buy new books for your Mac and use Apple Books to read and manage the books and audiobooks in your library. Make a goal for your reading and record the books you've read so far and the ones you still want to read.

Note: Not all nations or areas have access to Apple Books.

A bookshelf on your Mac: The top books in Reading Now are the ones you've begun reading. To find new books and other publications, browse or search through all of the materials in your library. Alternatively, click the Book Store or Audiobook Store link in the sidebar and select a category. Simply log in with your Apple ID (choose Account > login in) to make a purchase. Books can also be purchased directly from the search results page.

Set reading goals: Make reading a daily goal to inspire yourself to read more. If you want to aim higher, you may select a different target by clicking the **Adjust target button under Reading Now's Reading Goals section**. The default is 5 minutes every day. This can be disabled, and reading goal data can be cleared under the Books settings.

Add bookmarks, notes, and highlights: To add a bookmark to a page,

- drag your pointer to the top of the book you're reading to reveal the controls. Then, click the **Add Bookmark button** (click the bookmark again to delete it). Select the **Show Bookmarks button**, select **the bookmark**, and then **show the controls to access a bookmarked page.** Select the text, and then select a highlight color or Add Note from the pop-up menu to add notes or highlights. Show the controls and select the Notes and Highlights icon to view your notes at a later time.

Never lose your place or your markups: As long as you sign in with the same Apple ID on your Mac, iOS devices, and iPadOS devices, your purchased books, collections, bookmarks, highlights, and notes, as well as the page you're now reading, are instantly accessible on all of them.

Calendar

Calendar ensures you never miss an appointment. Organize your hectic schedule by making several calendars and managing them from one location.

Create events: To add a new event,

- double-click anywhere in the day, or click the **Add button**. Spotlight can also be used to swiftly add a new event. Double-clicking **the event, selecting Add Invitees, and entering an email address are the steps involved in inviting someone.** Calendar informs you when those you invited respond.

A calendar for every part of your life: Make distinct calendars, each with a different color, for things like jobs, schools, and homes. To make a new calendar, select **File > New Calendar.**

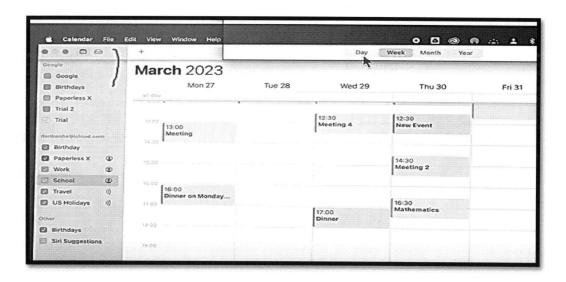

Then, Control-click on each calendar to select a different color.

Add holiday calendars: View international holiday calendars from various locations. Select the holiday calendar you wish to add by selecting **File > New Holiday Calendar.**

Filter your calendars with Focus: Select the calendars that will appear during a specific Focus. Have a calendar, for instance, that only illuminates when you are studying and has dates for assignments. Select **System Settings from the Apple Menu, and then pick Focus from the sidebar.** Click **the Right arrow after selecting a focus on the right, then select Add Filter from the Focus Filters menu.**

Share across your devices and with others: Your calendars are updated when you are logged into iCloud on all of your Mac computers, iOS devices, iPadOS devices, and Apple Watch that are linked to the same Apple ID. Calendars can be shared with other iCloud users as well.

FaceTime

Make audio and video calls to a friend or group of friends from your Mac using FaceTime. With FaceTime, you can also utilize your iPhone, iPad, and MacBook Air in new ways. For example, you can use your iPhone's camera as a webcam or transfer calls across the devices.

Make a FaceTime call: Initiate FaceTime video calls using your Mac's integrated FaceTime HD camera.

- After selecting **New FaceTime and entering the recipient's name, contact information (phone number or email address),** click **FaceTime.** If making a video call isn't convenient, you can make an audio-only connection by clicking the pop-up menu and choosing **FaceTime Audio**. You have the option to join a FaceTime session using both audio and video when you receive an invitation.

Hand off a FaceTime call: When you're not at home, initiate a FaceTime call on your iPhone, then transfer the call to your Mac when you return to your workstation. Alternatively, you can answer a FaceTime call from your Mac and move to a different device as needed. Your headphones also make the switch if they are connected to Bluetooth.

- Click **the video symbol in the Mac menu bar**, select **Switch**, and then select Join in the FaceTime window on your MacBook Air to transfer a FaceTime call from your iPhone or iPad to your MacBook Air. From your MacBook Air, to transfer a FaceTime call to your iPhone or iPad, simply hit the video symbol in the top left corner of the device, select **Switch**, and then touch **Switch again.**

Use your iPhone as a webcam: Use the iPhone camera's capabilities to make FaceTime calls from your Mac. Maintain your iPhone steady and in landscape mode, with the back cameras pointed in your direction and the screen off (you could even put it on a stand).

- Navigate to **FaceTime > Video on your Mac**, then pick your iPhone from the list. You can use Center Stage on iPhone 11 and later, which keeps the call focused on you when you move. This is made possible by the Ultra Wide camera.

Share your screen: You can quickly share one or more apps from the window you are in when on a conversation using FaceTime or another compatible video conferencing app.

- Click **Share on FaceTime while your cursor is over the Mission Control key in the upper-left corner of your window.** You may also use your shared screen to overlay your video. There are two overlays available: huge and mini. The small overlay places you in a movable bubble above your shared screen, but the large overlay keeps the focus on you by framing your screen next to you on a different layer. Select **the large or small option under Presenter Overlay after clicking the video icon in the menu bar.**

Show what's in front of you: You can share what's in front of you in addition to your face while using Desk View to use your iPhone as a webcam for your MacBook Air.

- Configure your iPhone as a webcam, and subsequently tap **Desk View in the upper right corner of the FaceTime window on your Mac to share with Desk View during a FaceTime chat.** You can also select **Desk View by clicking the Video icon in the navigation bar.** After aligning your desk with the window using the controls, select **Share Desk View.** Click **Close in the Desk View window** to end the sharing session. The iPhone 11 and later models support Desk View.

Note: You must have Continuity Camera enabled in AirPlay & Handoff configurations on your iPad or iPhone, and you must be logged into your MacBook Air, iPad, and iPhone using the same Apple ID in order to transfer a FaceTime call or utilize your iPhone as a webcam for your Mac. Bluetooth, WiFi, and Handoff must be enabled on your iPhone, iPad, and Mac.

Sign language recognition and Live Captions: When someone uses sign language, FaceTime recognizes it and highlights them during a group FaceTime session. FaceTime Live subtitles recognize speech and display subtitles for the active speaker in real time.

Watch and listen together: To view and listen together on a Mac, use SharePlay. Moreover, you can share your screen while on a FaceTime call. To begin, click the **SharePlay icon. Refer to "Connect with others."**

Note: To participate in SharePlay, some apps need to be subscribed to. Not every country or area has access to every feature or piece of information.

Make a phone call: Use FaceTime to make phone calls from your Mac to any iPhone running iOS 8 or later. Just make sure the feature is enabled on both your Mac and iPhone and that they are signed in with the same Apple ID account. (To use FaceTime on your Mac, launch it, choose **FaceTime > Settings, then click "Calls from iPhone."**)

Note: In order to make or receive calls on your Mac, your MacBook Air and iPhone need to be linked to the internet and the same Wi-Fi network.

FindMy

You can use the same software, Find My, to find your friends, family, and Apple gadgets.

Share locations with friends: To share your location with friends and family,

- Click the **Share My Location button in the People list**.

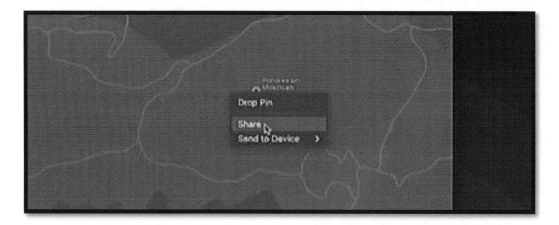

You can choose to cease sharing your real-time location at any time. You can choose to share for as long as a day, an hour, or forever. To see a friend's location on a map and receive detailed directions to it, you can also request to follow them.

Set location alerts: Notify pals automatically when you go to or from a particular area. Additionally, set up alerts for when your buddies come and go. You may see all of your friends' location-related notifications in one area by clicking Me in the People list and then navigating to Notifications About You.

Get informed when you leave anything behind: On your iPhone, iPad, or iPod touch, set up separation notifications to let you know when you've left your MacBook Air or other device behind.

- To configure a device to send out separation alarms, click **the Info icon, select Notify When Left Behind, and then adhere to the on-screen directions.**

Secure a lost device: To find and safeguard lost devices, including your Mac, iPhone, or AirPods, use Find My.

- To find a device on the map, click on **it from the Devices list.** When you click the Info button, you can choose to remotely wipe the device, mark it as lost to prevent others from accessing your data, or even make the device play a sound to help you find it.

Locate devices even if they are offline: In situations where your device is not linked to a Wi-Fi or cellular network, Find My leverages Bluetooth signals from other close Apple devices to find your device. These encrypted, anonymous signals assist in finding your lost smartphone without compromising your privacy. For Mac computers running macOS 12 or later, iPhones and iPod touch devices running iOS 15 or later, and iPads running iPadOS 15 or later, you can even locate an erased device.

Find everyday items: When you can't find something, like your keychain, attach an AirTag to it to help you find it quickly. To link an AirTag and compatible third-party products to your Apple ID, use your iOS or iPadOS device.

- On a Mac, locate an item by selecting **the Items tab in Find My and then clicking on the item in the list to see its location on a map.** In the event that the object cannot be found, you can see its most recent position and get a notification when it is. For an object that has a message and phone number on it, you can even activate Lost Mode.

Freeform

For collaboration and idea organization, use Freeform. Make a board and then fill it with text, images, files, and more. Work together and observe real-time changes.

Note: macOS Ventura 13.1 or later is compatible with Freeform.

Create a board: To start a new board, select the **New Board button on the toolbar.** Boards are automatically stored. Choose **Untitled in the upper left corner of the title bar and type a name to give a board a name.** Across all of your devices, your boards sync. Go to iCloud Settings and enable Freeform if your boards aren't syncing. iOS 16.2 and iPadOS 16.2 or later support Freeform.

Add text, media files, and more: To add text, files, links, sticky notes, and photographs to your board, use the toolbar. Additionally, you can drag objects from other apps onto your board.

Make a diagram: To make a diagram, use forms, lines, and other elements. After selecting View, select Show Connectors. You can add text, shapes, or sticky notes, for example, and then drag an arrow to make a connective line.

Collaborate in Freeform: You can copy and distribute the link, or you can use Messages or Mail to extend an invitation to work together on a board.

- Choose Collaborate by clicking the **Share button in the toolbar, then choose Messages, Mail, or Copy Link.** Everybody on the thread gets access to the board if you share in Messages.

GarageBand

You can compose, record, and share music with GarageBand. It's your very own home recording studio, complete with everything you need to learn how to compose music, record songs, and play an instrument.

Create a new project: You can begin by choosing a template for a song, changing the key, tempo, and other parameters, then clicking **Record to begin playing**. Compose a tune using various tracks and loops, for instance. To find out what things are and how they operate, click **Quick Help and move the cursor over them.**

Bring in the beat: With Loops, you can easily incorporate drums and other instruments into your production. To locate a loop by Instrument, Genre, or Descriptor, click the **Loop Browser**. Then, drag the loop into a vacant space in the Tracks section. With a straightforward set of settings, you may alter Loops to suit your song.

Record your voice: After selecting **Track > New Track**, go to Audio and choose the microphone. To configure input, output, and monitoring, clicks **the triangle next to Details, then select Create**. To begin or stop recording, click the **Record or Play buttons, respectively.**

Home

You can quickly and safely operate every HomeKit accessory from your Mac with the Home app.

Whole-house view: The revamped Home page allows you to quickly view every aspect of your house, including room-specific accessories, scenes, and cameras. To facilitate quick access, categories, and rooms are also included in a redesigned sidebar structure.

Accessory control: The Home app displays accessories as tiled icons. The color of the accessory categories makes them visually identifiable, and you can select which tiles to increase to make them stand out more on the Home tab. To operate an item, simply click on it. You can adjust the blinds, lock or unlock the door, turn on or off the lights, and more. Additionally, you can change a light's brightness or a thermostat's target temperature.

Categories: You can easily retrieve all the necessary accessories arranged by room with the help of the Lights, Climate, Security, Speakers and TVs, and Water categories, which also provide more thorough status information.

Activity History: Check who opened and closed the door, as well as when. Additionally, you may view the latest activity for security systems, contact sensors, and garage doors, among other accessories.

Create a scene: Set up a scenario where a single command can control all of your accessories working together. Make a Good Night scene, for instance, where you close the drapes, lock the door, and turn out all the lights before retiring for the evening. Click, and then select **Add Scenario to start a scenario.**

HomeKit Secure Video: Keep all of your home security camera footage on iCloud; it won't take up any space there. Set up activity zones that a camera can see to record footage or get alerts only when motion is detected there. Security cameras and doorbells that use Face Recognition may identify people you've classified as recent guests in the Photos or Home apps, in addition to detecting people, animals, packages, and vehicles. A compatible HomeKit-enabled security camera, an iCloud plan that supports HomeKit, and a HomePod, Apple TV, or iPad acting as a home hub are all needed for HomeKit Secure Video.

Adaptive lighting: To optimize comfort and productivity, program your smart light bulbs to automatically modify the color temperature throughout the day. Warm colors help you wake up, colder colors help you stay focused and alert throughout the daytime, and blue light helps you wind down at night. A home hub is necessary for adaptive lighting.

Add a widget: To access, monitor, and control home accessories, add a Home widget to your desktop. To access the Notification Center, click the date or time in the upper right corner of the screen. From there, select **Edit Widgets located at the bottom of your alerts**.

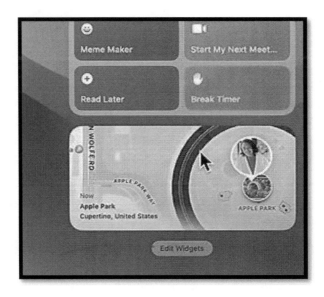

In the sidebar, select **a widget by clicking Home**. New widgets can be dragged to any location on your desktop or in the Notification Center.

iMovie

With just a few fast clicks, you can use iMovie to transform your home footage into stunning films and Hollywood-style trailers that you can share.

Import a video: You can import video from your Mac's media files, a camera, or your iPhone, iPad, or iPod touch. You get a new library and event created by iMovie.

Record video with the built-in camera: Record video with your Mac's FaceTime HD camera and use it into your project. To begin and end recording, select **an event from the sidebar**, click **Import in the toolbar**, choose **FaceTime HD Camera, and then click the Record button**.

Create Hollywood-style trailers: Create witty trailers with catchy tunes and animated visuals. All you have to do is modify the credits and add images and videos. Click the New button, select **Trailer, select a template from the Trailer window, and then click Create to get started**. In the Storyboard tab, upload your images and videos, and in the Outline tab, add the cast and credits.

Keynote

Use Keynote to create presentations that are innovative and professional. Choose from more than 30 pre-made themes to start, and then customize it with text, 3D elements, and a different color scheme.

Working together on a Keynote presentation and monitoring changes is now simpler than ever thanks to Activity Stream.

Organize visually: Slides can be added, rearranged, or deleted fast with the slide navigator on the left. You can drag a slide to reorder it, click **a slide to view it in the main window, or choose a slide and hit Delete to erase it.**

Collaborate in Messages: In Messages, you can extend an invitation to collaborate, and the Keynote presentation is automatically shared with all participants on the thread. Make sure Collaborate is chosen before clicking **Messages after selecting the Share option from the navigation bar. Select the group name that you wish to include among the participants.**

Work together in real time: Using Activity Stream, you can see revisions and comments made by contributors on a Keynote presentation in a comprehensive list located in the sidebar. Any modifications to the file management system or who has been included in the Keynote presentation can be easily followed.

Present in any situation: Utilizing an external monitor, make your in-person presentation while utilizing your Mac to view forthcoming slides, presenter notes, a timer, and a clock. Host a slideshow in a videoconference with other presenters, maintaining control just like you would in a solo presentation. Among other things, you can use your iPhone, iPad, or Apple Watch to remotely manage your presentation and create an interactive one that the audience may interact with.

Share your presentation: To send a copy of your presentation by mail, message, airdrop, or even social media, select **Share > Send a Copy.** This is useful if you want to communicate it with others on a conference call or if your boss wants to evaluate it.

Mail

With Mail, you can control every email account you have from a single app. Most widely used email services, including iCloud, Gmail, Yahoo Mail, and AOL Mail, are compatible with it.

Set up your email accounts: Are you sick of having to log into several websites just to check your email? To view all of your communications in one location, set up Mail to connect to all of your accounts. Select **Mail > Add Account.**

Manage your messages: View your inbox containing only the messages you want to see. Mail allows you to unsubscribe from mailing lists, silence excessively busy email conversations, and block messages from individual senders by moving them straight to the Trash. Additionally, you can restrict what messages in your inbox appear to be unread.

Send later and get reminded: Plan an email to be sent at the ideal time. Click the **drop-down menu next to the Send button when writing a message.** To customize a day and time, choose from the list of suggested dates or click **Send Later.** To be reminded about an email you opened but didn't respond to, you can also choose a time and date. To remind me of an email, **control-click on it in your inbox**. The message will appear at the top of your inbox again when you select when you would want to be reminded.

Undo send: Quickly retract a recently sent email before it enters the recipient's inbox. Within ten seconds after sending, click Undo Send in the Mail sidebar. The amount of time you have to delete an email is likewise customizable.

- To undo the send delay, navigate to **Mail Settings > Composing and select an option from the pop-up menu next to it.**

Find the right message: Enter your search term to view recommendations for messages that most closely match your inquiry. Mail has a built-in intelligent search function that looks for synonyms for the search terms you provide, returns more precise results, and detects typos. While you look for emails, smart search also lets you explore shared material thoroughly.

Never miss an email: To rapidly preview incoming messages, a notification flashes at the top-right of the screen when you receive new emails. (You don't want alerts? Navigate to System Preferences, select Notifications from the sidebar, and turn them off. To adjust your notification preferences, select Mail under Application Notifications on the right.)

Maps

Utilize a map or a satellite picture to find destinations and obtain directions. Use Apple's carefully crafted guidebook to find the top attractions in each city. To drop a pin at a location, force click on it.

Explore in detail: Maps provide additional information to aid in your exploration of the surrounding area, such as landmarks, altitude, and other natural characteristics. New city experiences on your Mac using Apple silicon provide elements like buildings, trees, and landmarks.

Plan your route: Plan your route, monitor traffic, and view road specifics such as turn and bus lanes with the updated driving map. Create routes with several stops, view them automatically on your iPhone, and send directions to a buddy via Messages in no time.

Find and save your favorites: Locate the information you seek and refine the outcomes. To find out vital details about a location, such as a business's opening hours or whether a restaurant accepts takeout, click on it. The locations you visit most frequently can be added to your favorites.

Discover new places with guides: With the help of carefully selected guidelines from reputable brands and partners, Maps makes it easy for you to find amazing locations to dine, shop, and travel the world; you can save these guides and receive updates whenever places are added.

See indoor maps for major destinations: Navigate certain airports and retail centers. Simply zoom in to discover nearby eateries, locate restrooms, arrange a meeting place with pals at the shopping center, and much more.

Get there on public transit: For some cities, Maps offers information about Nearby Transit, including scheduled departures close to you. To obtain recommended routes, transit costs, and an anticipated time of arrival, select a location from the sidebar and then click the Transit button. If your favorite transit routes are close by, pin them so they always appear at the top.

EV trip planning made easy: When you connect your electric car to your iPhone, Maps not only estimates your ETA but also indicates the locations of charging stations along the way.

Plan your cycling route: Maps provides you with the necessary information to plan your bike ride, including information on traffic patterns, height, and the presence of strong inclines. You can email your itinerary to your iPhone after you've planned it.

Messages

Messages make it simple to communicate, regardless of the device you're using. Handle group texts, quickly view stuff that others have shared with you, prioritize favorites, and much more. Using iMessage, you can text anyone who owns a Mac, iPhone, iPad, iPod touch, or Apple Watch. Alternatively, you can use SMS or MMS to text other people.

Unlimited messages with iMessage: You may send as many text messages, photographs, live photographs, videos, and other types of media as you like to anyone who has an iPhone, iPad, iPod touch, Mac, or Apple Watch when you log in with your Apple ID. These devices get encrypted communications from the communications app via iMessage, which shows up as blue bubbles in your discussions.

Send SMS/MMS: If your iPhone (running iOS 8.1 or later) is logged into Messages using the same Apple ID as your Mac, you can send and receive SMS and MMS messages on your Mac even if you're not using iMessage.

- To enable Text Message Forwarding on your iPhone, navigate to **Settings > Messages, select Text Message Forwarding, and then hit the name of your Mac**. If you are not utilizing two-factor authentication for your Apple ID, you will see an activation code on your Mac. On your iPhone, enter the code and select Allow. Messages sent by SMS and MMS show up in green bubbles during conversations and are not encrypted.

Unsend and edit messages: You can amend a freshly sent message up to five times within 15 minutes of sending it, or you can unsend a message up to two minutes after sending it when chatting in Messages. You can choose to Edit or Undo Send by controlling-clicking on any sent message.

Keep favorite conversations at the top: Drag and drop your preferred chats to the top of the messages list. Above a pinned chat, you may see typing indicators, tapbacks, and new messages. The most recent participants show up around the pinned conversation when there are unread messages in a group conversation.

Message group conversations: To facilitate group identification, designate a picture, Memoji, or emoticon as the group image. You can reply to a question or statement made earlier in the chat by adding your response as an inline reply. You can also use the keyboard shortcuts to type a person's name or swipe right on any message in a group conversation. You can conceal alerts related to a chat when it gets too lively.

- Select **the conversation from the list**, and then tap the Details button in the upper-right corner of the Messages window to view options for managing the conversation and establishing a group image. navigate to **Messages > Settings, select General, and tick the "Notify me when my name is mentioned" option to be notified when you are mentioned.**

Create your own Memoji: Create your own customized Memoji by selecting elements of your face, hair color and style, freckles on your skin, and more.

- Go to **Messages > Settings to set a customized Memoji as your Messages photo. Click "Name and Photo Sharing," then select "Continue," before selecting "Customize."** To customize your look, click the **New Memoji button** and then each feature. Once you're done, click **Done** to include the Memoji in your collection of stickers. To expand your Memoji collection, initiate a discussion, select Apps, then Stickers, then select **New Memoji, and then enjoy creating.**

Send a file, photo, or video: Drag and drop files into Messages to distribute them quickly can easily locate and share pictures and videos from your library of photographs.

  - To add a photo to a discussion, click the **Apps button, select Photos, and then click the photo**. To locate a particular photo, enter a phrase in the search field, such as the name, date, or location of the individual.

Find the right message: You can quickly refine your search and find the message you're looking for by combining search filters. You can quickly search your discussions using various parameters, such as a person or phrase, and view the results sorted into categories like messages, photographs, and talks.

Shared with You: You can enjoy content sent to you over Messages by individuals in your Contacts at any time; it will appear instantly in a new Shared with You area in the associated app. Content that has been shared with you can be found in the Apple TV app, Photos, Safari, Apple News, and Apple Podcasts. In addition to the shared content within the respective applications, you can view the sender of the content and click to launch the related conversation in Messages. This allows you to carry on the conversation while you're enjoying the shared content.

Collaborate on projects: To work together on files, Keynote presentations, Numbers spreadsheets, Page documents, Notes, etc., you can issue an invitation. Click the Share icon in the app you want to use for collaboration, confirm that Collaborate is chosen, and then select Messages. Select the name of the group you wish to include, and the document, spreadsheet, or any shared document will instantly include every member on the thread. You may see engagement notifications at the top of the Messages line whenever someone adjusts.

Filter your messages with focus: Just the messages you wish to see during a given Focus will be shown. Simply view discussions with people you typically play multiplayer games with, for instance, if you have a Gaming Focus.

- Select **System Settings from the Apple Menu, then pick Focus from the sidebar.** Click the **Right arrow after selecting a focus on the right, then select Add Filter from the Focus Filters menu.**

Music

Organizing and enjoying songs, albums, and purchases from the iTunes Store in both your personal collection and the Apple Music catalog—which offers millions of tracks for on-demand listening—is made simple with the help of the Apple Music app. Click to see the current song's lyrics, previously played songs, and what comes next. Browse the iTunes Store to find the music you desire.

It's in your library: You may quickly browse and listen to the music in your own library, purchases you made from the iTunes Store, and items you added from the Apple Music catalog. Sort your material by Artists, Albums, Songs, or Recently Added.

Browse the best of Apple Music: To view new and exclusive titles from Apple Music; a service for streaming music that requires a monthly subscription, click the Browse button on the sidebar. Discover the ideal mix for every occasion by choosing from a wide variety of playlists and over 50 million songs available for free streaming and download. You can begin following your favorite musicians to get updates on new releases as well as suggestions for other musicians you might like.

Tune in: To listen to Apple Music 1 live or any episode from the Apple Music family of shows, click **Radio in the sidebar.** Discover the range of stations designed for nearly all musical genres.

Listen together: With up to 32 buddies, utilize SharePlay to enjoy music in real-time. Initially, initiate a FaceTime call with the group and then select the **SharePlay option.**

- Click the **Play button** after moving the cursor over any song or album in the Music app to begin listening. All listeners simultaneously experience the same music, have access to common playback controls, and can rearrange or add songs to the shared music queue. Additionally, clever volume adjusts audio automatically so that you can still hear each other even in noisy areas.

Buy it on the iTunes Store: Click the iTunes Store link in the sidebar if you wish to purchase your music. (If you select Music > Settings, select General, and finally click Show iTunes shop, the shop should appear in the sidebar.) Whenever screen real estate is at a premium, use MiniPlayer to launch a tiny, movable floating window so you can use your Mac to listen to and manage music while you work on other tasks. Select **Window > MiniPlayer to launch MiniPlayer.**

News

Apple News is your one-stop shop for reliable, editor-curated, and uniquely tailored news and information. Articles can be bookmarked for offline or cross-platform reading at a later time. For a single monthly fee, you may read hundreds of publications, well-known newspapers, and premium digital publishers with Apple News+. The news feed makes it simple to browse and verify stories by including prominent bylines and publication dates. Save articles directly from the news feed for later reading or sharing. A more comprehensive search function and the News+ Library, which groups your content by magazines, downloadable content, newspapers, and catalog to make it simpler to access your favorites, are included in the package for News+ members.

Customize your feed: To see your preferred channels and subjects in the Today feed and sidebar, follow them. To follow a news source or topic, type it into the search area and click the **Add button.** Click **Add to Favorites after Control-clicking the channel to make it stand out more in the sidebar.**

Follow your favorite teams with My Sports: With My Sports, you can keep up with your preferred teams and leagues and read articles from regional newspapers, sports journals, and other sources. Highlights are available along with scores, schedules, and standings for the best collegiate and professional leagues. In the sidebar, click Sports to begin following your preferred sports.

Puzzles: You can tackle the daily crossword and crossword mini puzzles if you have an Apple News+ subscription. To begin playing a puzzle, click **Puzzles in the sidebar. Not accessible in every nation or area.**

Use Quick Note to save and organize articles: You have the option to annotate news stories with a Quick Note and tag them for future reference, ideal for when you're conducting research for a project or vacation. Fn-Q or a designated Hot Corner can be used in News to open Quick Note and save the article link.

The Notes app's sidebar is where you may locate the Quick Note later.

Notes

The best location to jot down brief ideas or store lengthy notes that include checklists, photos, connections to websites, and more is under Notes. Collaboration tools, including as activity view, mentions, and shared notes and folders, make it simple to collaborate with others and keep informed about changes made to your note. Additionally, you can utilize Smart Folders to automatically classify your notes depending on factors such as when the note was generated or changed, whether it contains checklists or attachments, and more. Tags can also help you stay organized. Additionally, iCloud makes it simple to maintain device syncing, allowing you to always have access to your notes on any device that you have signed in to with your Apple ID.

Add content, lock notes, and share them: To rapidly add checklists, images, videos, sketches, tables, links, and more to your note, use the Notes toolbar. To format text, such as adding a list, creating a heading, or styling text as a block quotation, click the Font button. To secure your note using your MacBook Air login password, click the **Lock button. Alternatively, you can set a unique password.**

- To share a note via **AirDrop, Mail, Messages, or Reminders, click the Share button, select Send Copy, and then select the desired sharing method.**

Collaborate on a note: You can copy and distribute the link, or you can send an invitation to work together on a message in Mail or Messages.

- Select **Messages, Mail, or Copy Link after clicking the Share icon in the toolbar and selecting Collaborate from the menu.** Everyone in the discussion is automatically added to the list if you post the link in Messages. By selecting the **Collaborate button,** you may monitor activity and control collaboration once you've asked others to participate.

Add links to other notes: Enter ">>" into a note to create a link to another note, then select the note you wish to link to from the list. If the note you're looking for isn't on the list, try typing its title until it does. Enter the new note's title and click "**Create Note" "[note title]" to establish a link to it. The notes list now includes the new note.**

Add tags: To classify and arrange the items in your note, use tags anywhere in the body of the text. After typing the # symbol, type the text for your tag. If you want to easily get to notes with a certain tag or tags (such as #travel or #cooking), you may view your tags in the sidebar. Using the same tags, Custom Smart Folders automatically gather notes in one location.

Use mentions: To get in touch with your project partners directly, add mentions (type @ followed by a name, like @Leslie) whether working on a project or in a social context. They can immediately join in and take part after receiving a notification that they have been referenced in a letter.

Add a Quick Note from anywhere: You can use Quick Note to take notes from any Mac app or website, which you can then examine in the Notes sidebar's Quick Notes category. Point your cursor to the lower-right corner of the screen, where Quick Note is available as a Hot Corner by default, to start a new one. You can also use the -Q keyboard shortcut.

Note: Select the **System Settings icon > Desktop & Dock, click Hot Corners, and select a corner to assign to a Quick Note in order to generate Quick Notes using a different Hot Corner.** To ensure that your Quick Note doesn't obstruct what you're viewing, you can resize or relocate it by dragging a corner or the title bar.

Numbers

Create visually appealing and functional spreadsheets on your Mac with Numbers. You can get started quickly when creating invoices, team rosters, budgets, and more with the help of over thirty Apple-designed templates. Microsoft Excel spreadsheets can also be opened and exported using Numbers. Working together on a Numbers spreadsheet and monitoring changes is now simpler than ever thanks to Activity Stream.

Start with a template-then include what you want: Type fresh text after selecting the template's example text. Drag a graphic file from your Mac onto the placeholder picture to add graphics.

Collaborate with Messages: Messages allow you to extend an offer to collaborate, and when you do, all participants in the thread are immediately added to the Numbers spreadsheet. Make sure Collaborate is selected by clicking the Share option in the navigation bar, and then picking Messages. Select **the group name that you wish to include among the participants.**

Get organized with sheets: To display alternative views of your material, use several sheets or tabs. Use one sheet for notes, another for a table, and a third for your budget, for instance. To add a new sheet, click **Add**. To rearrange the sheets, **drag a tab left or right.**

Formulas are a snap: Get built-in assistance for over 250 potent functions by just typing the equal symbol (=) in a cell to view a sidebar listing all the functions and their descriptions. Enter a formula to receive recommendations right away.

Choose the range of cells that contain the values to obtain instantaneous computations for a set of data. The selected values' count, minimum, maximum, average, and sum are displayed at the bottom of the window. To view even more options, click the **Menu button located at the bottom right.**

Create pivot tables: Using a table or range of cells in a spreadsheet as the basis for your data, create a pivot table that can be used to quickly categorize and summarize values, analyze any amount of data, and spot intriguing patterns and trends. In addition to adding and organizing pivot table data and creating a snapshot of the pivot table that you can transfer to other applications, you can also modify the cell range of your source data.

Pages

On your Mac, use the Pages software to create beautiful, multimedia-rich papers and books. Access and modify Microsoft Word documents, keeping track of both your own and other users' edits. It's now simpler than ever to work together on a Pages document and monitor changes as they happen thanks to Activity Stream.

Look good: It's simple to get started on a project using Pages' pre-made, professionally designed templates for books, newsletters, reports, resumes, and more.

Collaborate with messages: Messages can be used to extend an invitation to cooperate, and the Pages page is automatically updated with the names of all participants on the thread. Make sure Collaborate is selected by clicking the Share option in the navigation bar, and then picking Messages. Select the group name that you wish to include among the participants.

All your formatting tools in one place: To access the Format inspector, click the Format button located in the toolbar. The formatting options for anything you select appear in your document.

Become a publisher: With the book templates that Pages provides, you may make interactive books in EPUB format. Include a table of contents in addition to text and pictures. When you're prepared, you may publish your book on Apple Books for sale or download.

Translate in a snap: Choose the text that needs to be translated. Select the text with a control-click, select Translate, and then select a language. To insert text into another language, select "Replace with Translation." To work offline, you can download more languages by going to **System Settings, Language & Region, and clicking the Translation Languages tab at the bottom. Not every language is supported.**

Photos

Organize, edit, and share your images and videos using Photos and iCloud Photos. Ensure that your photo collection is current across all of your devices. Your best photos are shown under Photos, and you can easily find and enjoy your favorites with the help of more robust search capabilities. With simple editing tools, you can create expert-quality changes to your images and films. Additionally, you can now share an album with up to five other people via iCloud Shared Photo Library. Everyone may contribute images and videos, arrange and comment on the album, and take pleasure in each other's edits.

All your photos on all your devices: You can browse, search through, and share every picture and video from every device that is logged in with the same Apple ID using iCloud

Photos. Any photo you take with your iPhone shows up automatically across all of your devices. Additionally, any photo editing you do gets synced across all of your devices.

- Start by navigating to **System Settings, selecting your Apple ID from the sidebar, selecting iCloud, and finally turning on Photos.**

Set up iCloud Shared Photo Library: To make sure that everyone in the family has more full memories, share pictures and movies in a different library. Your photos and content from the Shared Library coexist harmoniously in the Photos app. All members of the library are notified when someone uploads, edits, or removes a photo or video from the shared library. One shared library that is accessible to you and up to five other individuals can be used. You need to have iCloud Photos turned on and be logged in with your Apple ID to set up the iCloud Shared Photo Library.

- Select **Get Started after selecting the Shared Library tab under Photos > Settings.** You have the option to add participants immediately or at a later time. Choose which of your previous images and videos—all of them, ones with specific individuals, ones taken after a specific date, or a manually selected selection of images and videos—you wish to add to the Shared Library. You can switch between seeing your Personal Library, the Shared Library, or both libraries simultaneously in Photos once the Shared Library is configured.

Add photos and videos to your shared Library: You can Control-click a picture or video in your Library and select "Move to Shared Library" to transfer it to your Shared Library. To utilize recommendations for images or films that you might wish to contribute,

- navigate to **Photos > Settings, pick the Shared Library tab, check Shared Library Suggestions, and select "Add People" to get recommendations for images or movies featuring particular individuals.**

Shared with You: Photos sent to you via Messages by friends in your Contacts automatically show up in the Shared with You area of your Photos app. Your library contains pictures of events you attended and other things you're probably interested in. You can open Messages and carry on the conversation by clicking the message bubble on a photo while viewing them in the Photos app.

Edit like a pro: Effortlessly edit photographs and videos with robust yet user-friendly editing tools. You may make quick edits to your photo or video by using the editing buttons above it.

- Click **Edit for more advanced editing options, and use Smart Sliders for polished outcomes. Both images and movies can be cropped, rotated, exposed more, and filtered.**

Interact with text: On your computer and online, Live Text can identify text contained in photographs. On a Mac, you can click a picture to call a phone number or visit a website, or you may copy text from a photo and paste it into any file.

- Select the **text, Control-click it, and then select Translate to translate it. Not every language is supported.**

Find what you are looking for: Photos display the best images from your collection while concealing screenshots, receipts, and duplicates. To rapidly explore your full collection of images, click All Images. Alternatively, use the buttons at the top of the Photos window to view photos by year, month, or day. You may search your photographs based on what's in them when they were taken, who you mentioned in them, the captions you added, and, if given, their location. Photographs recognize items, scenes, and people in your images and videos. Spotlight and Siri can also be used for photo searches.

People, places, and things: Several things in your images can be recognized using Visual Lookup. The information button or swipe up on a picture can be used to highlight scenes and things that you recognize. Find out more about literature, flora and flowers, pets of different breeds, popular art, and global landmarks.

- Click the **Favorites icon** that shows up on the photo of the person you want to have their photo always be at the top of the People album. View all of your images with location information on an interactive map by using the Places album. You can enlarge a map to see additional images taken at a certain spot.

Become Creative with Live Photos: You may use the Loop effect with Live Photos to play the animation back and forth or continually loop the action. Use Long Exposure to blur motion in your Live Photos to create a professional DSLR look and transform an everyday waterfall or running stream into a piece of art.

Podcasts

On your Mac, browse, subscribe to, and enjoy your favorite podcasts with Apple Podcasts. Your personalized suggestions let you find new podcasts categorized by subjects that interest you.

Get started with Listen Now: Get the most recent episodes of the podcasts you subscribe to in one location, along with tailored suggestions for podcasts you might find interesting. Any podcasts you're currently listening to—even ones you started on a different device—are preserved in Listen Now while you're logged in with your Apple ID.

Discover new podcasts: Use Listen Now to discover podcast recommendations based on topics and shows, or use Top Charts to see which shows are currently popular. If you find a show you enjoy, either download the episode to your library or sign up for the podcast. Based on your interests, you'll see recommendations from your friends in Shared with You and receive recommendations for related subjects and television programs.

Save episodes to your library: Click the Add button to add a single episode to your library. Click Subscribe to receive updates whenever a new episode of a podcast is released. Click the Download icon to save a podcast for offline listening.

Follow your favorites: To ensure that you never miss a new episode, click **Follow to add a show to your favorites. Check out the latest additions to your library's Recently Updated section.**

Preview

With the Preview app, you can read and edit PDFs and photos, annotate PDFs, convert graphic file types, batch edit files, password-secure PDFs highlight and translate text, and much more. You can even fill out and sign forms online.

Fill in a PDF form: Select a field in the form in Preview, and then enter your text there. To save the form, open it at a later time, and proceed with filling it out, select **File > Export.**

Save a PDF with a password: Give a password to a PDF so that users can't access the contents without it. Open the password-protected PDF in Preview,

- Select **File > Export, and then click Permissions**. Choose Permissions from the menu, and then enter the Owner Password password. To confirm, type it again, select **Apply,** and then select **Save.**

Add and remove PDF pages: You can add, remove, or rearrange pages in a PDF by opening it in Preview.

- Add a page: Choose **Edit > Insert, choose the page you wish to appear before the new one, and then select either "Page from File" or "Blank Page."** The existing page is put before the new one.
- Delete a page: pick the page or pages you want to remove by selecting **View > Thumbnails or View > Contact Sheet, then hit the Delete key on your computer (or pick Edit > Delete).**
- **Move Pages**: Select **View > Contact Sheet or View > Thumbnails, then drag the pages to reposition them.**
- Copy a page from one PDF to another: Select **View > Thumbnails or View > Contact Sheet in each PDF,** then drag thumbnail photos to move them from one to the other.

Translate in a snap: Choose the text that needs to be translated. Select the text with a control-click, select **Translate, and then select a language.** To work offline, you can download more languages by going to System Preferences, Language & Region, and clicking the Translation Languages tab at the bottom. Not every language is supported.

View and convert image files: Images can be converted by Preview to a wide range of file formats, such as JPEG, JPEG 2000, PDF, PNG, PSD, TIFF, and more.

- Select **File > Export, click the Format option, select the file type, enter a new name, select the file location, and click Save while the image is open in Preview.** Holding down the Option key while you click the Format menu can allow you to view specialized or older formats if you don't find the option you desire.

However, take note that if you want to convert many image files at once, open each file in a separate window, select all of them using the Command-A keyboard shortcut, and then proceed as directed above. By selecting every picture file and

- Selecting **Tools > Adjust Size**, you may easily resize image files in bulk.

Reminders

Keeping track of all your to-do lists is now easier than ever thanks to reminders. Make reminders for anything you want to keep track of, such as work projects, grocery lists, and other tasks. To arrange your reminders to fit your workflow, use adaptable tools like Custom Smart Lists and Tags. You can also store your reminder lists as templates so you may use them again at a later time. To cooperate and work together, you may also share a list with other people.

Add and edit a reminder: To add a new reminder, click the **Add button** in the upper right corner or the area beneath the list of reminders. To your reminder, add tags, notes, and a date or location. To add further information, click t**he Information button**. For example, you can add an early reminder to get another notification when an important event happens.

Create Custom Smart Lists: Your future reminders are automatically sorted by Smart Lists according to dates, times, tags, places, flags, or priority. Click **Add List, choose "Make into Smart List," and then add filters to create custom smart lists.**

Create grocery lists: The goods you add to grocery lists are automatically sorted into areas such as Meat, Produce, and Snacks & Candy. Click **Add List and select Groceries from the List Type pop-up menu to make a grocery list.**

See what's coming up: The items in the sidebar's Today and Scheduled lists are arranged according to the time and date. Stay aware of impending reminders so you don't miss a beat.

Organize your reminders: To make a reminder become a subtask, drag it over another reminder or click **it and hit Command-]**. To maintain a clear picture, you can expand or collapse your subtasks. To put related reminders in one section, add one to your list. If you would like to add another section, select **Manage Sections > Add Section or Edit > Add Section**. Click the **placeholder reminder at the bottom of the area and begin typing to add a reminder.**

To arrange reminder lists in the sidebar of a group, select **File > New Group**. You can give the group whatever name you choose. You can drag lists into and out of the group to add or remove items.

Collaborate on a list: You can share the link or send an invitation via Messages or Mail to work together on a list. After selecting Messages, Mail, or Invite with Link, click the Share button. Everybody on the thread is instantly added to the list if you share in Messages. By selecting the Collaborate button, you may monitor activity and control collaboration once you've asked others to participate.

Assign responsibility: Those with whom you share lists can be notified by setting reminders. Assign responsibilities to each person and make sure they are all aware of their roles. Select the **Share icon** in the menu that appears and select the sharing option to share a list.

Get reminder suggestions in Mail: Siri may identify potential reminders when you're corresponding with someone in Mail and offer suggestions for you to create them.

Quickly add a reminder: To add a reminder quickly, use natural language. For instance, to make a recurring reminder for that day and time, enter "Take Amy to soccer every Wednesday at 5 PM."

Safari

Safari is a potent and effective browser that offers cutting-edge privacy safeguards like passkeys. As long as you log into iCloud using the same Apple ID, you can access your tab bar, extensions, and start page from anywhere you browse—on your Mac, iPhone, and iPad.

Start searching: Enter a word or the address of a website, and Safari will display webpages that match and those that are recommended. Alternatively, you can pick one item from your Safari start page that you like or use often. Click the **Add button on the extreme right of the Safari window, or use Command-T**, to open a new tab and begin a new search.

See tab contents quickly: Favicons, which are website-associated emblems or icons, in tabs make it easy to quickly identify a webpage. To view a preview of the contents of a webpage, move the pointer over it.

Keep your browsing separate with profiles: To segregate your history, favorites, Tab Groups, and more; create distinct profiles in Safari, such as School and Personal. Navigate to **Safari > Create Profile selects New Profile**, give the profile a name, and add a symbol, color, and additional customizations. Select the **Add button to create a new profile if you've previously made one**.

Organize with Tab Groups: You can make a Tab Group for the websites you wish to keep together when conducting research for a project or trip.

- Click the **Add Tab Group icon and select New Tab Group to create a group from the tabs that are currently open when the sidebar icon is active.** To generate a new Tab Group by combining some of your open tabs, choose each tab you wish to include in the group by clicking on it, and then select the **Add Tab Group icon.**

In Messages, you can extend an invitation to work together on a Tab Group, and all participants in the thread are immediately added to the Tab Group.

- To share a Tab Group, click the **More Options icon in the sidebar,** select **Share Tab Group, and then select Messages.** Colleagues can add their tabs to a Tab Group once it has been shared, and you can see which page other members of the Tab Group are currently on.

You can access your tabs from anywhere with the same Apple ID on devices that are connected to iCloud thanks to Tab Groups.

Find out about extensions: With extensions, you may customize your browsing experience by adding new features to Safari. There are extensions available to help you with language correction, ad blocking, discount searching, and fast content saving from your favorite websites.

- To browse the App Store's Safari extensions category, which includes featured Safari extensions and categories (such as Browse Better, Read with Ease, Top Free Apps, and so forth), select **Safari > Safari Extensions. Once you have extensions, go to Safari settings and enable them. To enable extensions, select the Extensions tab and tick the checkboxes.**

Turn your favorite websites into web apps: You may easily access and monitor website notifications by saving a website to the Dock. Navigate to the website in Safari, hit the Share button, and then select **Add to Dock from the menu on the far right of the window.** This will build a web application. Click **Add after putting in a name.**

Browse the web safely: Whenever you open a website that isn't secure or that might be attempting to deceive you into disclosing personal information, Safari alerts you. Additionally, Safari protects you from online tracking and increases the difficulty of fingerprinting your Mac. By locating and eliminating the data that trackers leave behind, Intelligent Tracking Prevention combats cross-site tracking by utilizing the most recent advancements in machine learning and on-device intelligence.

Enjoy your privacy: Click **File > New Private Window** to open a private browsing window. Your private window locks when you close it and needs to be unlocked with your login or Touch ID. Safari won't remember your browser history when you use private browsing. It also helps stop websites from tracking you, fully prevents known trackers from running on pages, and eliminates tracking that is used to identify you from URLs while you surf.

- Click the **Privacy Report icon** to the left of the active tab to see the cross-site trackers Safari is blocking on each website, so you can get a better idea of how a site handles your privacy. To view a privacy report containing additional information about the trackers that are currently in use on the website, select the **Full Report button.**

Conceal your email address: When filling out a form on a website, for instance, or any other occasion where you need a distinct email address, you can establish as many as you like with an iCloud+ subscription. Emails sent to the Hide My Email address you create for a website are routed to your email account. Email can be sent and received without revealing your real email address, and you can disable your Hide My Email account at any moment.

Shortcuts

With a single click or by launching Siri, you can rapidly do multi-step tasks using the Shortcuts app. Make shortcuts to transfer text across apps, find directions to the next appointment on your calendar, and more. To run many steps in a process, use pre-made shortcuts from the Shortcuts Gallery or create your own by combining different programs.

A gallery of possibilities: Browse the Gallery or do a quick search. There are sets of starter shortcuts available for a variety of frequently performed tasks. The Gallery sidebar's My Shortcuts section displays the shortcuts you create as well as any pre-made shortcuts you select or modify. Click the **Sidebar to display or hide the Gallery sidebar.**

Build custom shortcuts: To get the desired outcome, create a new shortcut and then drag activities from the selection on the right to the shortcut editor on the left. Like steps in a process, actions are the building pieces of a shortcut. You can select from a variety of activities, such as copying the present web address from Safari, making a folder, or obtaining the most recent photo from the Photos app. additionally, you can employ script-running operations like rounding numbers, putting airplane mode on, and performing calculations. Additionally, Shortcuts offers "next action" recommendations to assist you in finishing your shortcut.

Sync and share shortcuts: Use the same Apple ID to log into all of your devices, and your shortcuts will be visible across them. Your other devices automatically update with changes you make on one. It's also possible to exchange shared shortcuts with other users and accept shared shortcuts from them.

- Double-click the shortcut, select **"Share," and then select the preferred method of sharing. In the sidebar of the Share Sheet, you can also create shortcuts to perform frequently used tasks.**

TV

Use the Apple TV app to watch all of your movies and TV series. Purchase or rent films and television series, sign up for channels and resume watching from all of your devices.

Get started with Watch Now: Explore a carefully selected feed of suggested content in Watch Now, which is based on the TV series, and movies you've viewed and the channels you subscribe to.

Discover more in Movies, TV Shows, and Kids: To find what you're searching for, select the Movies, TV Shows, or Kids tab from the menu bar and then narrow down your search by genre.

See what your friends are sharing: You can view episodes and movies that your friends and family share with you using the Messages app whenever it's convenient for you. Simply search for them in the Apple TV app—under the new Shared With You section of Watch Now. Only when the sender is listed in your Contacts will content appear in Shared with You.

Watch together: FaceTime may be used to connect with pals, and SharePlay can be used to watch a movie or TV show with friends and family. You can even use Messages to share comments while you're watching. Click the Play button after dragging the pointer over any item in the TV app to begin watching. You may use your iPhone to talk with pals while viewing stuff on your Mac. Additionally, the smart volume automatically adjusts the audio so that even in noisy environments, you can still hear each other.

Note: You must have iPadOS 15.4 or later and macOS version 12.3 or later on your iPad to use SharePlay. To play with certain SharePlay-compatible apps, you must have a subscription.

Not every country or area has access to every feature or piece of information.

Voice Memos

Recording voice memos of class lectures, interviews, song ideas, and personal reminders is now simpler than ever. You may use iCloud to access voice memos that you record on your iPhone directly on your MacBook Air.

Record from your MacBook Air: To begin recording, click the **Record button**; to end recording, click the **Done button**. A recording can be renamed to make it more recognizable. After selecting the default name, type a new one. Press the **Play button to hear your recording played back.**

Organize with folders: Make folders to aid in the organization of your voice memos. Select the Sidebar button and then the New Folder button located at the sidebar's bottom to add a new folder. After giving the folder a name, click **Save**. Holding down the **Option button** while dragging a recording into the folder allows you to add it.

Skip silence: Fill in the silences in your audio. To enable Skip Silence, click the **Playback Settings button located at the top of the Voice Memos window.**

Change the playback speed: Adapt the audio to your speed. Toggle the slider left or right after selecting the Playback Configuration icon at the top of the Voice Memos window.

Enhance a recording: Minus background noise and room reverberation, and your voice memos will sound better. To activate Enhance Recording, click the **Playback Settings option** located at the top of the Voice Memos window.

Using apps in full-screen

You may utilize every square inch of the screen and eliminate desktop distractions by using the full-screen mode that many Mac apps offer.

- You may utilize every square inch of the screen and eliminate desktop distractions by using the full-screen mode that many Mac apps offer.
- In the full-screen, get any of the following done;
  - **Show or hide the menu bar**: Pointer movement can be either toward or away from the screen's top. The menu bar is always visible if you have deselected the option to conceal it and show it in full screen mode.
  - **Show or hide the Dock:** The Pointer can be moved to or from the Dock's location.
  - **Move between other apps in full screen**: Depending on how you have your trackpad settings configured, swipe left or right with three or four fingers.
  -
- To exit the full-screen application, either click the button or move the pointer back to the green button. From the menu that displays, select **Exit Full Screen.**

You can maximize the window to operate in a larger window without going full screen; the menu bar and the Dock stay visible as the window expands. You can rapidly select another app to use in Split View if you're using an app that takes up the entire screen. To access Mission Control, use the Control-Up Arrow key (or swipe up with three or four fingers). Then, drag a window from Mission Control onto the Spaces bar's full-screen app thumbnail and click **the Split View thumbnail.** In the Spaces bar, you may also drag the thumbnail of one program onto another.

Using apps in Split View

Split View, which allows you to work with two apps side by side at once, is supported by a lot of Mac software.

- To shift the Tile Window to Left or Tile Window to Right of Screen menu on your Mac, move the pointer to the green button located in the upper-left corner of the window.
- Click the second program you wish to use, which is located on the other side of the screen. A new desktop area is used to generate the Split View.

- **Perform any of the subsequent actions in Split View:**
  - To reveal or conceal the menu bar, drag the cursor towards or away from the screen's top. The menu bar is always visible if you have deselected the option to conceal it and show it in full-screen mode.
  - Drag the pointer to or away from the Dock's location to reveal or conceal it.
  - Show or conceal the toolbar and title of a window: After clicking the window, drag the pointer toward or away from the screen's top.
  - To enlarge one side, move the pointer over the center separator bar and drag it to the left or right. Double-click the separator bar to get the sizes back to as they were before.
  - To flip a window, use its toolbar and title to drag it to the opposite side.
  - Switch to an alternate app on one side: To replace the tiled window, click the program window, move the cursor over the green button in the upper-left corner, select Replace Tiled Window, and then click the desired window. Click the desktop to go back to the current window if you choose not to replace it.
  - Click the app window, move the cursor over the green button in the upper-left corner of the window, and select Move Window to Desktop to move the window to the desktop. The desktop version of the app is shown. To access the app that was in Split View, press **Control-Up Arrow or slide up using three or four fingers to access Mission Control.**
  - Once there, click the app in the Spaces bar to bring it back to full-screen mode.
  - Use the full-screen app window: After clicking the application window, select **Make Window Full Screen by dragging the mouse over the green button located in the upper-left corner of the window.** To access the app that was in Split View, press Control-Up Arrow or slide up using three or four fingers to access Mission Control. Once there, click the **app in the Spaces bar to bring it back to full-screen mode.**

You can rapidly select another app to work with in Split View if you're using an app that takes up the entire screen. To access Mission Control, use the Control-Up Arrow key (or swipe up with three or four fingers). Then, drag a window from Mission Control onto the Spaces bar's full-screen app thumbnail and click the Split View thumbnail. In the Spaces bar, you may also drag the thumbnail of one program onto another. Make sure the "Displays have separate Spaces" option is enabled in the Desktop & Dock settings to use programs in Split View on other monitors.

Install and reinstall apps from the App Store

Installing and uninstalling apps that you bought with your Apple ID can be done in a few different ways. It should be noted that all of your App Store purchases are linked to your

Apple ID and cannot be changed to a different Apple ID. To view all of your store purchases on this Mac and download any available updates, always sign in with the same Apple ID when making purchases on your iPhone, iPad, or another Mac.

Install apps that you purchased on another device

Any software that you have purchased using your Apple ID can be installed on a different device.

- Click your name in the lower-left corner of the Mac App Store, or click **Sign In if you** haven't already.
- Find the app you purchased and click the **"Download"** button to start the download.

Reinstall apps

You can reinstall any software that you bought with your Apple ID if you uninstalled or erased it.

- Click your name in the lower-left corner of the Mac App Store, or click **Sign In if you** haven't already.
- To reinstall a paid app, find it and click the **Download button.**

Install and uninstall other apps

You can reinstall any software that you bought with your Apple ID if you uninstalled or erased it.

- Click **your name** in the lower-left corner of the Mac App Store, or click **Sign In if you** haven't already.
- To reinstall a paid app, find it and click the **Download button.**

CHAPTER 9

CUSTOMIZE YOUR MAC

Change System Settings

You may personalize your Mac by adjusting the system settings. You can select a light or dark appearance, alter the background, and do a lot more. Your Mac's options are arranged under settings. For instance, the Appearance settings have the Accent and Highlight color settings.

- Either select **Apple menu > System Settings** or select the **System Settings symbol in the Dock.**
- Select a setting by clicking. Based on your Mac and the installed apps, the settings are displayed in the sidebar and may change.
- Modify a choice.

For additional information on the options, most settings have a Help button that can be clicked. You must perform one or more steps if the System Settings icon in the Dock displays a red badge. For instance, the Dock icon displays a badge indicating that you haven't finished configuring iCloud functions. Clicking the icon brings up the settings, allowing you to finish the configuration. To modify the settings of an application, such as Mail or Safari, launch it, and select **Settings from the menu bar by clicking the app's name. Certain apps don't have settings.**

Choose your desktop wallpaper

The image that appears on your desktop can be changed. Use your photographs or pick from a selection of Apple-provided images or colors.

- Select **System Settings** from the Apple menu on your Mac, and then select **Wallpaper from the sidebar. (You might have to scroll below.)**
- **Choose a background image from any of the accessible categories:**
  - Add Photo, Add Folder, or Add Album: This allows you to select your pictures.
  - Dynamic wallpapers: These pictures change color according to the time of day where you are right now.
  - Aerials of landscapes, cities, underwater scenes, and the earth: these still photos display striking vistas.
  - Shuffle Aerials: You can adjust the interval at which these still photos change.
  - Images: These still photos display imaginative imagery.
  - Colors: You can set solid-colored desktop wallpaper with these swatches.

- Configure your wallpaper. The wallpaper you select will affect your options. As an illustration, you can:
  ○ Set your wallpaper still picture to playback in slow motion as a screensaver.
  ○ Decide on how frequently to skip over commercial breaks.
  ○ Select the Dynamic Wallpaper in either light or dark still form.
  ○ Include your color.

To set an image as your wallpaper, drag it from your desktop or a folder into the Wallpaper settings thumbnail at the top. Open the Photos app, choose a photo, select the Share icon in the Photos toolbar, and then

- Select **Set Wallpaper to immediately use that shot.**

Another option is to set an image from the internet as your wallpaper. In the browser window, control-click the image and choose **Apply Image as Desktop Picture.**

Add and customize widgets

To monitor your schedule, favorite devices, weather, top news, and more on your Mac, add widgets to the desktop or Notification Center. Choose the date and time in the menu bar or use two fingers to slide left from the right edge of the trackpad to launch Notification Center. Select wherever on the desktop to end it. Click the wallpaper to make the open windows go away so you can view your desktop widgets if they are hidden by other windows. You can set the Desktop & Dock settings "Click wallpaper to reveal desktop" to Only in Stage Manager if you don't want the open windows to go away when you click the desktop. Once you've done this, you can only use Stage Manager by clicking the desktop to close windows.

Add widgets to the desktop

- Control-click the wallpaper on your Mac, then select Edit Widgets.

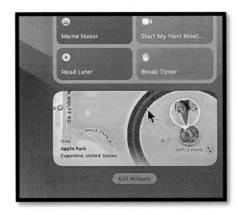

- Look through the widget gallery to find a widget. Or select a category to see the widgets that fall under it.
- **You can perform any of the following to add widgets to the desktop:**
    - Place a widget on the desktop automatically: Select the widget (or the Add button on the widget).
    - Place a widget on the desktop by hand: On the desktop, drag the widget to any desired location.
    - Drag the new widget to a different spot on the desktop to adjust its position. Click the Remove button on the new widget if you determine you don't want it.
- Click **Done** in the widget gallery's lower-right corner once you've completed adding widgets.

Add widgets to the Notification Center

- Launch Notification Center on your Mac.
- Click **Edit Widgets at the Notification Center's bottom.**
- Look through the widget gallery to find a widget. Or select a category to see the widgets that fall under it.
- Take any of the following actions to add widgets to the Notification Center:
    - Move the widget to the desktop's upper-right corner.
    - Select the widget (or the Add button on the widget).
    - Drag the new widget up or down in the Notification Center to adjust its position. Click the **Remove button** on the new widget if you decide you don't want it.
- Click **Done in the lower-right corner** of the widget gallery once you've completed adding widgets.

Use iPhone widgets on your Mac

For your iPhone to utilize widgets from installed apps, it has to be:

Utilizing iOS 17 or a later version

Logged in using the Apple ID associated with your Mac

On the same Wi-Fi network as your Mac, or close to it

- Select **System Settings from the Apple menu on your Mac, and then select Desktop & Dock from the sidebar. (You might have to scroll below.)**
- Navigate to **Widgets and activate "Use iPhone widgets."** Now that your iPhone widgets are accessible in the widget gallery, you may use them to customize the desktop or Notification Center.

The program isn't installed on your Mac if you click a widget and get the message "Open [app name] on your iPhone to continue." To interact with the app, you have to open it on your iPhone. Not all third-party apps are compatible with Mac and iPhone.

Remove widgets from the Notification Center

- Launch Notification Center on your Mac.
- **Take one of the subsequent actions:**
  - To remove a widget, control-click on it and select **Remove Widget from the shortcut menu.**
  - Point the cursor over the widget you wish to delete, and then hit the **Remove button while holding down the Option key.**

Remove widgets from the desktop

- Click the wallpaper on your Mac, and then select **Edit Widgets.**
- For the widget you want to delete, click the **delete button.**

Use a screen saver

When you need more privacy or while you're not using your Mac, you can use a screensaver to hide the desktop.

Customize the screen saver on your Mac

- Select **System Settings** from the Apple menu on your Mac, and then select **Screen Saver from the sidebar. (You might have to scroll below.)**
- Choose a screen saver from the following categories:
  - macOS: The pictures are in slow motion.
  - Aerials of landscapes, cities, underwater scenes, and the earth: these slow-motion photos display breathtaking vistas.
  - **Shuffle Aerials**: You can customize the interval at which these slow-motion photos change.
  - Other: You can display a message, view a "Word of the Day," and more with your unique screensavers and photographs.
- **Configure your screen saver. The screen saver you select will affect your options. As an illustration, you can:**
  - Utilizing the slow-motion aerial of your screen saver, turn on a still aerial for your wallpaper.
  - Decide how frequently to cycle through the ads.
  - Select a style to help you navigate through your photos.

Start or stop the screensaver on your Mac

- After you set the duration of inactivity, the screen saver will launch automatically anytime your Mac is inactive. Choose **Apple menu > System Settings**, then select **Lock Screen** in the sidebar to adjust the amount of time your Mac can be idle before the screen saver activates. (You might have to scroll below.)

When you move the pointer over a hot corner that you've configured for the screen saver, the screen saver will launch instantly. Another way to launch the screen saver is to select Lock Screen from the Apple menu.

- You can use the mouse, the trackpad, or any key to bring up the desktop and end the screen saver.

Add a user or group

If you have many users on your Mac, you should create separate accounts for each so that users can customize settings and preferences independently of one another. Occasional users may check in as guests with no access to the data or settings of other users. Additionally, you can make groups on your Mac that contain the user accounts. To complete these activities on your Mac, you must be an administrator.

Add a user

- Select **System Settings** from the Apple menu on your Mac, then select Users & Groups from the sidebar. (You might have to scroll below.)

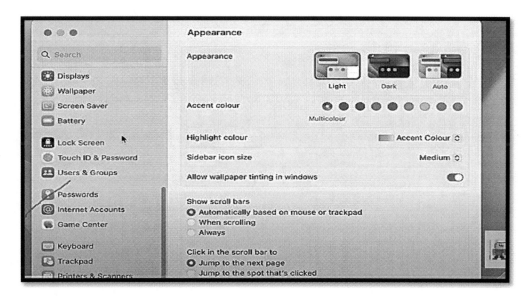

- Under the users list on the right, select the **Add User option (you may be prompted to provide your password).**

- Select a user type by clicking the New User pop-up menu.
    - **Administrator:** Installing apps, managing users, and making changes to settings are all possible for an administrator. When you first set up your Mac, it creates a new user who is an administrator. Administrators might be several on your Mac. It is possible to make new ones and elevate regular users to administrator status. Don't configure an administrator's login to be automated. Should you do so, someone may easily restart your Mac and obtain administrator access. Don't share administrator identities and passwords to protect your Mac.
    - **Standard:** An administrator creates standard users. Standard users are limited to installing programs and modifying their settings; they are unable to add or modify other users' preferences.
    - **Sharing Only:** Users with sharing-only access can remotely browse shared files, but they are unable to access the computer's settings or log in.
- For the new user, enter their entire name. An automatic account name generator is used. You cannot alter your account name after you have entered it.
- Enter the user's password once, then enter it one more for confirmation. To aid the user in remembering their password, enter a clue.
- Select "**Create User.**"

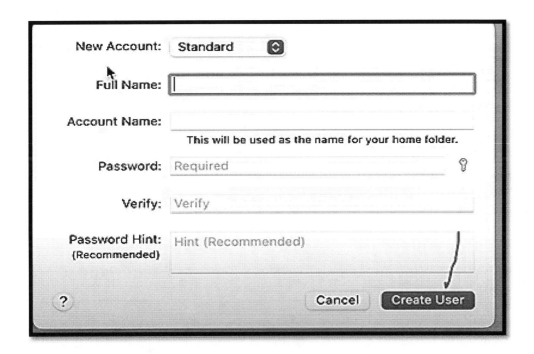

- If desired, expand on the user's capabilities. After selecting the Info option next to the user's name, take one of the following actions:
  - "Allow users to reset their password using Apple ID" should be selected. The user has to have iCloud set up on this Mac to use this option. The Guest User account and FileVault accounts, which enable users to reset their passwords using their Apple IDs upon startup, are not eligible for this feature.
  - Turn on "Allow users to administer this computer" to elevate a regular user to the position of administrator.

Create a group

Several users can share the same access privileges by creating a group. For instance, you can give a group exclusive access rights to a file or folder, to which all group members can gain access. Each of your shared folders can also have access privileges assigned to it specifically for a group.

- Select **System Settings** from the Apple menu on your Mac, and then select **Users & Groups** from the sidebar.
- Press the **"Add Group" button**. (You might have to scroll below.)
- After selecting the **New Group option** and giving the group a name, click **Create Group.**

- After selecting a group by clicking **the Info button,** users will become enabled in the resulting list.

You might need to adjust the File Sharing, Screen Sharing, or Remote Management settings to allow new users to share your files and screen.

Add your email and other accounts

By linking the accounts to your Mac, you can use Exchange, Google, Yahoo, and other online accounts in Mac apps. Internet Accounts settings are where you add internet accounts and control account settings. Certain apps allow you to add internet accounts as well. Internet Accounts settings display an iCloud account that you add through iCloud settings in Apple ID settings. Its settings are modifiable from either location.

Add an account from an app

Direct account addition is possible via the Calendar, Contacts, and Mail applications. The Internet Accounts settings display the accounts that you add through these apps. You have to register for an account on the provider's website before you may add one from an app.

- Click the name of the app in the menu bar on your Mac, then select **Add Account.** For instance, select **Mail > Add Account in Mail.**
- After choosing the account provider, click **Proceed.** Choose **Other [Type of] Account, click Continue**, and then provide the required account information to add an account from a provider that isn't listed, like a mail or calendar account for your business or school. Contact the account provider for information if you are unsure.
- Enter the needed information together with your password and account name.
- A dialog box where you can choose which apps to use with the account shows when you add an account that may be used by numerous apps.

Add an account in Internet Accounts settings

You have to register for an account on the provider's website before you can add it to the Internet Accounts settings.

- Select **System Settings** from the Apple menu on your Mac, and then select Internet Accounts from the sidebar.
- On the right, select **Add Account.**

Next, select the account provider's name. Click **Add Other Account**, select **the account type you wish to add,** and then **input the necessary account details** if you want to add an account from a provider that isn't mentioned, like a mail or calendar account for your business or school. Contact the account provider if you're unsure about the account type or its details.

- Enter the needed information together with your password and account name.
- A dialog box where you can choose which apps to use with the account shows when you add an account that may be used by numerous apps.

Automate tasks with Shortcuts

Check out the Shortcuts app's Gallery to find new shortcuts to add to your collection or to learn more about the possibilities and construction of specific shortcuts.

Open and browse the Gallery

- Go to the sidebar of the Shortcuts app on your Mac and select Gallery. Selected shortcuts are arranged in rows according to categories (such as Essentials, Morning Routine, etc.).
- Click **See All** to view every shortcut in a category.
- To view additional shortcuts inside a category, side-scroll the category row.
- To view more category rows, scroll **up or down**.

Add a Gallery shortcut to your collection

- Select **Gallery** in the sidebar of the Shortcuts app on your Mac, then select a **shortcut**. The shortcut's description appears.
- Click the **More Button** to receive a preview of the activities included in the shortcut. Click **Done** to go back to the description.
- Click **Add Shortcut** to add the shortcut to your collection.
- If the shortcut requires further setup, click **Add Shortcut after following the on-screen directions**. You now have the shortcut in your collection of shortcuts.

Search the Gallery

Additional shortcuts not displayed in the Gallery can be found by searching.
- Select **Gallery** in the sidebar of the Shortcuts app on your Mac, then type a search query into the upper-right corner search field. Below are shortcuts that correspond with your search query.

Create Memoji

You can make a customized Memoji that expresses your personality using macOS 11 or later. Next, send a Memoji to let your messages reflect how you're feeling.
- Pick any discussion in the Messages application on your Mac.
- To the left of the text box, click the **Apps button**. Next, click the **Stickers button**. Finally, choose the **Memoji button**.

- To build and personalize your Memoji, click the **Add or More buttons.** Then, follow the on-screen directions to change your Memoji's skin tone and entire body.
- Press "**Done.**"

Change your login picture

On your Mac, you can alter the image that shows up in the login window. In addition, your Apple ID picture and My Card in Contacts both feature your login photo.

Note: A checkbox on the user's photo indicates that you are unable to alter the picture for another user who is presently logged in. To make changes, the user needs to either log out or log in and modify their photo.

- Select **Users & Groups** in the sidebar after selecting **Apple menu** > **System Settings on your Mac.**

- Click the image to the right of your login name, and then take one of the following actions:
  - Choose a Memoji: To choose and compose a facial image, click **Memoji and then click the Add button**.

- Alternatively, pick a Memoji from the list and choose a preferred stance and style.
  - Choose an emoji: To choose an image from the emoji collection, select **Emoji, and then hit the Add button**. Alternatively, pick an emoji from the list and choose a style.
  - Choose a monogram: After choosing a backdrop color and **clicking Monogram, type your initials.**
  - Grab a photo with your Mac's camera: Press **the camera**. After lining up your shot, press the **Camera button**. You can take the picture again as often as necessary.
  - Choose an image from your library of photos: Select **Pictures**. To view images from a certain album, click **on the desired album, then pick a picture.**
  - Choose one of the suggested images: Click **Suggestions and pick an image.**

- You can change an image's appearance after you've chosen it. Take one of the following actions:

  - Modify the image's location: Move the image within the enclosed area.
  - Drag the slider to the left or right to zoom in or out.

- Press **Save**.

Change the system language

You can select a different language to use, even though your Mac is configured to display the language of the nation or region in which it was purchased. You can configure your Mac to use French, for instance, if you purchased it in the United States but do most of your work in that language. Additionally, you can select several languages for distinct apps. You can use a particular program in English, for instance, even if your system language is set to Simplified Chinese. This page can be viewed in a different language if you're using a web browser like Safari. Navigate to the bottom of the page, and select a country or region from the list by clicking on its name in the lower-right corner.

- Select **System Settings** from the Apple menu (the second option on the menu) on your Mac. Next, select **General from the sidebar and Language & Region from the list on the right**.

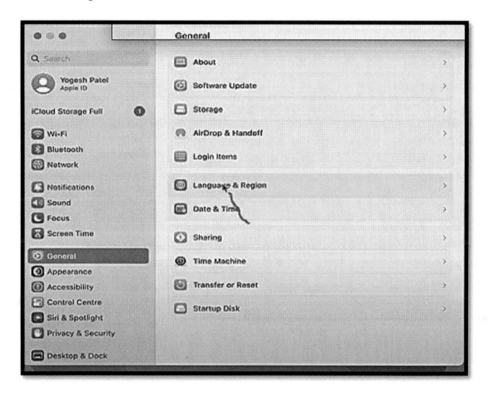

- **Choose one of the following actions under the list of preferred languages at the top:**
  - To add a language, click the **bottom-right button labeled "Add,"** choose the desired language from the list, and then click "**Add**." A separator line divides the list. The languages that are displayed in menus, notifications, webpages, and other places above the line are system languages, which macOS fully supports. Although macOS doesn't completely support languages below the line, some websites and programs you use may. A list of accessible input sources appears if you haven't already added one so that you can type in the language you're adding. You can add an input source in the keyboard settings at a later time if you don't add one now.
  - Modify the language used as the primary: Move a language to the front of the list of languages. Note: To view the update in all applications, you might need to restart

your Mac. To restart your computer, click Restart Now (the button with red lettering on the right). The user interface appears in the primary language if macOS, an application, or a website supports it. The following language in the list is used if the current language isn't supported, and so on. When you input characters in a script that contains characters from multiple languages, the order of the languages in the list impacts how the text looks.

Select the Settings pop-up menu and select Apply to Login Window if you want all users on your Mac to see the language you selected as the default language in the login window. (If the Settings pop-up menu isn't shown, the primary language is already selected in the login window.)

Choose the language you use for individual apps

- Select **System Settings** from the Apple menu on your Mac, then click **General in the sidebar before selecting Language & Region on the right**.
- Select **Applications** and take one of the following actions:
  - App language selection is as simple as clicking the Add button, selecting the desired app and language from the pop-up menus, and then clicking Add.
  - Modify an application's language from the list: After selecting the app, a pop-up menu will appear; select a new language.
  - Take an application off the list: After choosing the app, press the Remove option. Once more, the program speaks in its default tongue.

You might need to close and reopen the application if it's open to notice the change.

Make text and other items on the screen bigger

If the application is open, you may need to close it and then open it again to see the update. If the application is open, you may need to close it and then open it again to see the update.

Make everything on the screen bigger

You can increase the size of everything on the screen by adjusting the resolution of your display.

- Select **System Settings** from the Apple menu on your Mac, then click **Displays from the sidebar**.

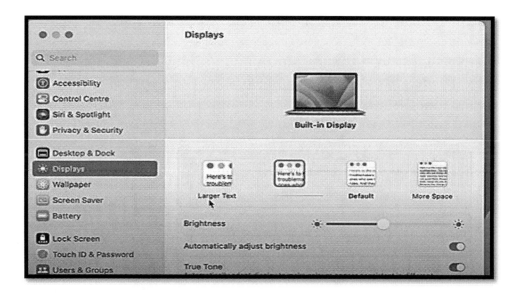

- Make a resolution selection on the right. All the elements on the screen are larger when the resolution is decreased.

Make text and icons bigger across apps and system features

To change the preferred text reading size in different programs, on the desktop, and in sidebars, all you need is one slider.

- Select **System Settings** from the Apple menu on your Mac, then select **Accessibility** from the sidebar. (You might have to scroll below.)
- On the right, select **Display**. Next, select **Text**. Finally, select **"Text size."** (You might have to scroll below.)
- If the listed apps are set to **Use Preferred Reading Size**, you can raise the font size on the desktop, in sidebars, and in them by dragging the slider to the right. Select the **pop-up menu beside the program, select a different text size, and that's it for any of the listed apps.**

Note: An app's settings have a unique text size set if it is set to Customized in App. The text size customization you specify within the program is replaced if you make changes to the text size in System Preferences.

Make text bigger for individual apps or system features

You may change the text's reading size within a lot of programs. Desktop sidebars and labels both have text size adjustments available.

- Within apps: You can use the Command-Plus (+) or Command-Minus (–) keys to change the text size when reading emails, messages, and articles in Mail, Messages,

155

and News, among other apps. Additionally, you may utilize System Settings to designate a preferred text reading size for specific apps, such as Messages, Calendar, and Mail.

- On webpages: To change the text size in Safari, use Command-Option-Plus (+) or Command-Option-Minus (–).
- In the Finder's file and folder names: Select **View > Display View Options**.

Select a text **size by clicking the "Text size" pop-up menu. Note: In Gallery view, text size cannot be altered.**

- Regarding desktop labels: Select the **"Text size"** pop-up menu by Control-clicking the desktop, and then select Show View Options.
- Sidebars: Select **System Settings from the Apple menu, and then click Appearance (you may need to scroll down).** Select **Large from the pop-up option that appears next to "Sidebar icon size" on the right.**

Activity

- Change the wallpaper on your desktop.
- Include widgets and also customize the ones you are using already.
- Use a screensaver on your desktop
- Add your email and other accounts to your Mac.
- Create a Memoji

CHAPTER 10
USING APPLE DEVICES TOGETHER

Work across devices using Continuity

Continuity allows you to work more efficiently and fluidly across all of your Apple devices when you use your Mac in conjunction with them. Use the same Apple ID to log in to all of your devices to utilize Continuity features. Your devices must also meet system requirements and have Bluetooth® and Wi-Fi enabled.

AirDrop

With AirDrop, you can easily and wirelessly exchange contacts, images, movies, and anything else with people nearby. It's as easy as dragging and dropping to share on your Mac, iPhone, iPad, and iPod touch.

AirPlay to Mac

You can use your Mac's screen to share, play, or display material from another Apple device.

Auto Unlock and Approve with Apple Watch

Without entering a password, use your Apple Watch to gain access to your Mac or accept requests for authentication from your Mac.

Continuity Camera

Utilize your iPhone as a webcam on your Mac, or use your nearby iPhone or iPad to snap a photo or scan a document, and it will instantly show up on your Mac.

Continuity Markup

You may use Markup tools on your Mac to write and draw on a PDF document or image, and you can view the changes instantaneously on your Mac. You can even use the Apple Pencil on your iPad to annotate and doodle on the page.

Handoff

Start an email, message, or document on one device, then continue where you left off on another. Apps including Mail, Safari, Calendar, Contacts, Pages, Numbers, Messages, Reminders, and Keynote are compatible with Handoff.

Instant Hotspot

Not even WiFi? Not an issue. When your iPhone or iPad is within range of one another, you can use their hotspot to connect your Mac to the internet without any configuration needed. To activate your hotspot, simply select your iPhone or iPad from the Wi-Fi menu on your Mac.

Phone Calls

Use your Mac instead of your iPhone when you want to make or take calls. Numerous programs, including FaceTime, Contacts, Safari, Mail, Maps, and Spotlight, allow you to initiate calls. You receive a notification when someone calls. To respond, simply click the notification.

SMS Messages

Using your Mac, you can send and receive SMS and MMS text messages. You can reply to text messages from friends using the nearest device, no matter what phone they own. Every communication that shows up on your iPhone also shows up on your Mac.

Universal Clipboard

On one Apple device, copy text, graphics, photos, and videos. On another Apple device, paste the copied material. For instance, you can copy and paste a recipe from your Mac's Safari into Notes on your nearby iPhone.

Universal Control

You can make use of a single keyboard and trackpad, or a linked mouse, to operate across multiple Macs or iPads when they are close to one another. Even content may be dragged between them. For instance, you can use the Apple Pencil to doodle on your iPad and then take it to your Mac to include in a Keynote presentation.

Use iPhone as a webcam

Utilize the potent iPhone camera and extra video effects by using Continuity Camera to use your iPhone as your Mac's webcam or microphone. You have the option of connecting wired or wirelessly using a USB cord.

You must complete the following tasks before you may use the Continuity Camera feature:

- Ensure that iOS 16 or later is installed on your iPhone and macOS 13 or later on your Mac.
- Note: You must have iOS 17 on your iPhone and macOS 14 on your Mac to use all of the Continuity Camera features.
- Utilizing the same Apple ID, log into both devices.
- Activate Bluetooth® and Wi-Fi on both devices.
- Verify that the gadgets you have meet the system's needs.
- Affix your iPhone.

Use your iPhone as a webcam or microphone

- Open any app on your Mac that can access the camera or microphone, such as Photo Booth or FaceTime.
- Select your iPhone to use as the camera or microphone from the app's menu bar or settings. Your iPhone launches the Continuity app, which starts streaming audio or video to your Mac from the back camera. Note: Your iPhone must be stationary, in landscape orientation, with the screen off, to be used as a microphone on a Mac without a built-in camera. As an alternative, you can use a USB cord to connect your iPhone to your Mac.
- **Do any of the following;**
  - To pause the audio or movie on your iPhone, swipe up to unlock it, or hit Pause.
  - Resuming the music or video on your iPhone requires tapping the Resume button. To lock it, hit the **Sleep/Wake or side buttons.**
  - Give up using your iPhone as a microphone or webcam: Close the application on your Mac.
  - Eliminate your iPhone as a choice: Select **Disconnect on your iPhone**, then confirm that you want to disconnect. Apps' listings of cameras and microphones as well as Sound Settings' list of sound input devices no longer include your iPhone.

Automatically switch to the iPhone camera

Certain Mac applications, such as FaceTime and Photo Booth, can immediately convert to using your iPhone as a camera input. Your iPhone has to be able to:

- Keep your Mac near at hand.
- Turn off its screen.
- Orient yourself in a landscape.
- Make sure the back camera or cameras are unobstructed and facing you.
- Not flat on a desk, not in a pocket
- Stay still.

Other Mac apps might also recognize your iPhone as the preferred camera if you've previously used it as a webcam on your computer.

Make your iPhone the default microphone

You may set your Mac's default microphone to be your iPhone.

- Select **System Settings from the Apple menu on your Mac**, and then select **Sound from the sidebar**.

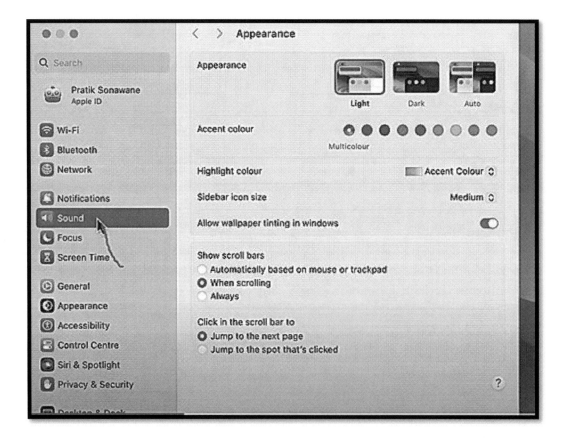

- From the list of sound input devices, pick your iPhone. Your iPhone launches the Continuity app and begins recording sounds.

160

Use iPhone with Desk View

Desk Observing with FaceTime and other apps lets you observe your desk from above and project your face simultaneously when using your iPhone as a webcam. There's no need for a complex setup.

Note: iPhone SE is not compatible with Desk View; it is only available with iPhone 11 or later.

Use Desk View with FaceTime

- Launch the **FaceTime app on your Mac.**
- Utilize your iPhone as a webcam by using a stand accessory to connect it to your Mac.
- Select the **Desk View icon** in the upper-right area of the video window after starting your video call. When the Desk image opens, a top-down image of your desk appears, simulating an overhead camera.

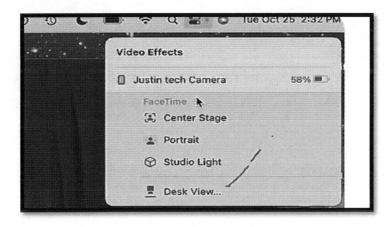

- Align your workstation with the camera using the workstation View setup box. Drag the onscreen control located at the window's bottom to adjust the zoom level. Click **Share Desk View** to begin sharing your desk view during the video conversation.
- Desk View can be disabled by selecting **Close Window (or Desk View > Quit Desk View** from the menu bar) after clicking the Screen Share icon in the upper left corner of the Desk View window.

Use Desk View with other apps

- Open a video-capturing app on your Mac.
- Utilize your iPhone as a webcam by using a stand accessory to connect it to your Mac.

- Select **Desk View after selecting the Video icon from the menu bar.** When the Desk image opens, a top-down image of your desk appears, simulating an overhead camera.
- Align your workstation with the camera using the workstation View setup box. Drag the onscreen control located at the window's bottom to adjust the zoom level. Select **Desk View when you're prepared.**

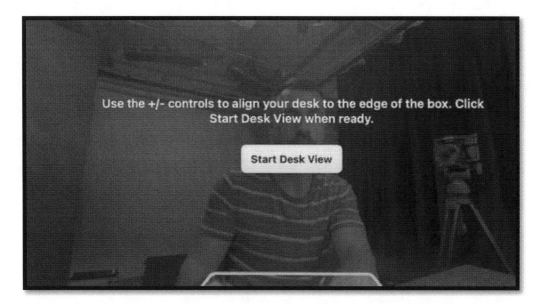

- Use the screen sharing option in the third-party app to choose the Desk View window to share what's on your desk. Check out the developer's instructions or browse the menus and settings of the application to learn how.
- Close the **Desk View window** or select **Desk View > Quit Desk View from the menu bar to disable Desk View.**

Stream audio and video with AirPlay

With AirPlay, you can wirelessly broadcast media from your Mac to your preferred speakers (like the HomePod mini), your Apple TV, and some smart TVs across a Wi-Fi network. Ensure that your Mac and all other devices are connected to the same wireless network.

Listen to music on your favorite speakers

Stream music from your Mac to one or more HomePods or any other AirPlay 2-capable speaker to get that big band sound.

- Launch the **Apple Music app** on your Mac, queue up some music, and select a speaker from the playing controls by clicking the **AirPlay audio icon**.

Play movies and more on the big screen

Playing videos, TV series, and movies on your TV's large screen is simple. Open the Apple TV software on your Mac, launch the show, and pick your Apple TV or smart TV from the playback controls by clicking the AirPlay video icon.

Share photos with everyone in the room

Everyone in the room can watch whatever's playing on your Mac, such as a slideshow of wedding images from the images app, on your large-screen TV thanks to AirPlay mirroring and your Apple TV.

- Choose your **Apple TV or smart TV by clicking Control Center in the menu bar on your Mac**, then clicking **Screen Mirroring**.

Use one keyboard and mouse to control Mac and iPad

With Universal Control, you may use a single keyboard, mouse, and trackpad to operate on up to three devices (such as a Mac and an iPad). Moreover, you can drag objects between devices.

Before using Universal Control, confirm the following:
- You're utilizing an iPad and Mac computer that is compatible.
- You are running macOS 12.3 or later on your Mac, and iPadOS 15.4 or later on your iPad.
- All of your devices have two-factor authentication enabled, and you are logged in with the same Apple ID.
- Both in System Settings (on your Mac) and in Settings (on your iPad), you have turned on Wi-Fi, Bluetooth®, and Handoff.

Connect your Mac to another Mac or iPad to use Universal Control

Using Universal Control, you may link your Mac to a neighboring device and operate across the devices with a single keyboard, mouse, and trackpad.

Note: You might need to reestablish the connection if you don't use Universal Control for a while.

Take one of the subsequent actions:

- To navigate the pointer to the right or left border of the Mac screen, use your mouse or trackpad. Move the pointer past the border that shows at the edge of the Mac screen to where it appears on the other device.
- Select **System Settings from the Apple menu on your Mac, then click Displays from the sidebar. (You might have to scroll below.) Select a device by clicking the Add Display pop-up option on the right, located beneath the Link Keyboard and Mouse. To make the pointer appear on the other device, slide it past the Mac screen's edge using your mouse or trackpad.**
- On your Mac, select a device beneath "Link keyboard and mouse to" by clicking **Control Center in the menu bar,** then select **Display.** To make the pointer appear on the other device, slide it past the Mac screen's edge using your mouse or trackpad.

Which side of the display you use to connect your devices depends on the direction in which you move the pointer during the connecting process. By rearranging the devices in the Displays settings, you can modify this behavior. After clicking **the display image, drag it to the desired location.** Any adjacent Mac or iPad can be programmed to automatically reconnect to your Mac. Select System Settings from the Apple menu, and then select Displays from the sidebar. (You might have to scroll below.) Select "**Automatically reconnect to any nearby Mac or iPad**" after clicking the Advanced option on the right.

Disconnect your Mac from another device

When you use Universal Control to link two devices, the connection lasts until you detach the devices or one of them goes to sleep.
- Select **System Settings** from the Apple menu on your Mac, and then click **Displays from the sidebar.**
- On the right, choose your display, and then select **Disconnect.**

Handoff between devices

You may start an application on a Mac, iPhone, iPad, or Apple Watch, and then pick it up on another Apple device with ease thanks to Handoff. Take the scenario when you begin responding to an email on your iPhone and complete it in Mail on your Mac. Numerous Apple programs, including Calendar, Contacts, Pages, and Safari, are compatible with Handoff. Apps from other parties might also function with Handoff. Your Apple devices must meet the Continuity system requirements to use Handoff. Additionally, they need to be enabled for Wi-Fi

Bluetooth® and Handoff in both Settings (on your iOS and iPadOS devices) and System Settings (on your Mac). All of your devices need to have your Apple ID signed in. Using Universal Clipboard, you can copy and paste text, pictures, photos, and videos between devices while Handoff is enabled. Additionally, files can be copied across Mac computers.

Turn Handoff on or off

Note: Your device will not function with Handoff if it does not have an option for Handoff.

- Using a Mac: Navigate to the **System Settings menu**, select **General** from the sidebar, select **AirDrop & Handoff** from the menu on the right

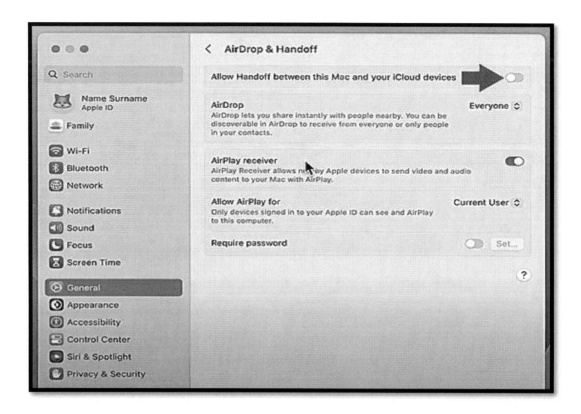

- And then select whether to enable or disable "Allow Handoff between this Mac and your iCloud devices." (You might have to scroll below.)
- Using an iPod touch, iPad, or iPhone: Select **AirPlay & Handoff under Settings > General,** and then toggle Handoff on or off.
- On Apple Watch: Launch the Apple Watch app on your iPhone, select **My Watch > General,** and then toggle the On/Off switch for Enable Handoff.

Handoff between devices

- From an iOS or iPadOS device to your Mac: On your iPhone, iPad, or iPod touch, the Handoff symbol of the Mac program you're using will show up at the bottom of the app switcher or the end of the Dock. To carry on using the app, tap.
- From an Apple Watch, iOS, or iPadOS device to your Mac: Near the right end of the Dock (or the bottom, based on the Dock position) on your Mac is where you'll find the Handoff icon for the program you're using on your iPhone, iPad, iPod touch, or Apple Watch. To carry on using the app, click the symbol.

To move to the app that bears the Handoff icon, you can also hit Command-Tab.

Unlock your Mac with Apple Watch

Without entering a password, you can utilize your Apple Watch to unlock your Mac or authorize app requests when it's close to your Mac when it's on.

Note: To take advantage of these features, you must have your Mac close to hand, your unlocked Apple Watch on, and two-factor authentication enabled for both your Apple ID and Mac (models mid-2013 or later).

Turn on Auto Unlock and Approve with Apple Watch

- Select **System Settings** from the Apple menu, and then select **Touch ID & Password from the sidebar. (You might have to scroll below.)**
- Navigate to Apple Watch on the right, then select the setting next to your watch's name. Only Apple Watches running watchOS 6 or later have access to this option.

Unlock your Mac

You can wake your Mac from its sleep mode by opening the display on a Mac laptop or by pressing any key on the keyboard. The screen lets you know that unlocking your Mac is happening.

Approve app requests

Your Mac will send an approval request to your Apple Watch when an app on your Mac needs authentication, such as to access passwords, unlock notes or settings, or authorize program installations.

- Select **Apple menu > About This Mac, click More Info, and then select System Report** at the bottom of the panel if you're unsure if your Mac endorses Auto Unlock and Approve with Apple Watch. Click **Wi-Fi in the Network part of the sidebar, then check for "Auto Unlock: Supported" on the right.**

As long as their Apple ID has two-factor authentication and their Apple Watch has the necessary version of watchOS installed, you can log in to another user's user account on your Mac and enable Auto Unlock or Approve with Apple Watch on their behalf if you are the administrator.

Make and receive phone calls on your Mac

You can use your Mac to make or receive phone calls instead of reaching for your iPhone. When someone calls, a notification shows up on your Mac, allowing you to answer it and, if your carrier allows it, use Real-Time Text (RTT) for calls.

Make phone calls from apps on your Mac

- Ensure FaceTime is turned on and sign in to the FaceTime app on your Mac.
- If you haven't previously, configure your Mac and iPhone for phone calls.
- Choose one of the following actions, depending on which macOS program you wish to use for your phone call:
  - ○ **FaceTime**: Select **New FaceTime**

Type a phone number into the pop-up window, hit **Return**, and then select **the number to call by clicking the downward arrow**. You can enter the person's name or choose them from Suggested if they have a card in the Contacts app. You have the option to place an RTT call if you have set up RTT phone calls.

Note: You may also send an SMS message to someone to invite them to a call.

- ○ Contacts: Click the **Phone button** after selecting a contact and dragging the pointer over a phone number. You have the option to place an RTT call if you have set up RTT phone calls.
- ○ **Safari**: Select **Call** after clicking a phone number on a webpage.
- ○ **Mail:** To make a call, hover your cursor over a phone number in an email, click the pop-up menu, and select your preferred method of communication.
- ○ On a map, select an area of interest and then select **Call.**

- Spotlight: Type a person or place's name into the search area, then select one of the suggested searches to see it in Spotlight. Click the Phone button after moving the pointer over a phone number.
- Calendar: Click on an event, then select **Call after finding a blue phone number that is underlined in the event description.** Alternatively, click Join to add a FaceTime video call to a calendar event.
- Reminders: Select a blue phone number that is underlined, click **Call, and then open the list of reminders.**
- Locate My: Choose a name after opening the People list. After selecting **Contact, Info, and Call,** click **Place a Call.**

Answer phone calls on your Mac

When a notification shows up in the upper-right corner of your Mac's screen, choose one of the following actions from the notification:
- Click **Accept** to answer an incoming call. Click **RTT** if you wish to answer the call using Real-Time Transcript (RTT) if the caller has configured it for you.
- Click **Decline to end a call.**
- Reject a call and use iMessage to deliver a message: Select **Reply** with reply from the drop-down menu by clicking **the arrow next to Decline, enter your reply, and hit Send**. The caller and you both need to be logged into iMessage.
- Turn down a call and make a note to call back later: To set the time for when you wish to get a reminder, select **the down arrow next to Decline.** When the time comes, a notification appears on your screen. Select it to view the reminder, and click **the link to initiate the call.**
- You can accept, reject, refuse, and send a message, or decline and set a reminder using the Touch Bar on your Mac.
- A call from someone who is blocked from communicating with you via ScreenTime cannot be answered, but it will show up as a missed call in the Notification Center or the FaceTime window.

Activity

- Use your iPhone as a webcam.
- Use your iPhone with Deskview
- Use a keyboard and mouse to control both your Mac and your iPad if you have one.
- Make and receive phone calls on your Mac.

CHAPTER 11

APPLE ID AND ICLOUD

Manage Apple ID settings

All Apple services, such as the App Store, Apple Music, iCloud, iMessage, FaceTime, and more, are accessible to you with your Apple ID. You can modify your personal information, security and sign-in preferences, payment and shipping details, and more using Apple ID settings after logging in with your Apple ID.

- Select **System Settings** from the Apple menu on your Mac, and then select [your name] in the sidebar's upper section. Click "**Sign in with your Apple ID**"

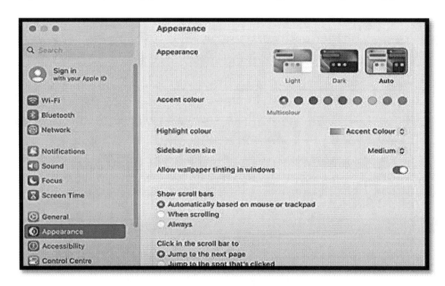

   If your name isn't displayed, then enter your password after entering your Apple ID and any other email addresses or phone number that is on file. You can create an Apple ID if you don't already have one.
- To control your Mac's associated Apple ID settings, select any of the following:
  ○ **Personal Information**: You can modify the name, birthday, and photo linked to your Apple ID using these settings.
  ○ **Sign-In & Security**: Make changes to your Apple ID's trusted phone numbers, contact details, password, and security settings using these options.
  ○ **Payment & Shipping:** Make changes to the shipping address linked to your Apple ID or view the payment method using these choices.

170

- o **iCloud:** Utilize these settings to manage iCloud storage, choose which iCloud functions to utilize, and activate iCloud+ capabilities.
- o **Media & Purchases**: Make changes to your subscriptions, account preferences, and download and purchase requirements by using these options.
- o **Family Sharing:** You may share your subscriptions, purchases, location, and more with up to five family members by using these options to create and administer a Family Sharing group.

Set your Apple ID picture

As your Apple ID picture, you can choose from a picture, Memoji, emoticon, or other image. In addition, the image associated with your Apple ID appears as the background for your My Card in Contacts and as your user login picture on Mac computers.

- Select **System Settings** from the Apple menu on your Mac, and then select [your name] in the sidebar's upper section. Click **"Sign in with your Apple ID"** if your name isn't displayed, then enter your password after entering your Apple ID and any other email address or phone number that is on file. You can create an Apple ID if you don't already have one.
- Select "**Personal Information.**"
- Click **Edit next to "Memoji, photo, or monogram." The possibilities for the Apple ID photo appear.**
- Get any of the following done;
  - o Choose **a Memoji by clicking Memoji in the sidebar,** selecting an animated GIF or Memoji from the list that appears, or clicking **the Add button**, choosing and customizing face features and other elements like clothes, and then clicking **Done**. To select the desired pose for your Memoji or Animoji, click **Pose**. To change the background color, click **Style.**
  - o To choose an emoji, either click the **Emoji button in the sidebar,** click one of the emoji that is presented, or click the Add button. After choosing a backdrop color, click **Style.**
  - o To choose a monogram, click **Monogram in the sidebar,** type in up to two initials, and choose **a background color.**
  - o Using your Mac's camera, snap a photo: After positioning your shot and selecting Camera from the sidebar, click the **Camera button.** You can take the picture again as often as necessary.
  - o Choose an image from your library of photos: Choose a photo by clicking on Photos in the sidebar. Click **Albums in the sidebar**, choose a picture, and you will see images from that particular album.

- - Choose one of the suggested images: Choose a photo by clicking the Suggestions link in the sidebar.
- Once you've chosen an image, you can modify its appearance using the sidebar's options for any of the following:
  - Modify the image's location: Move the image within the enclosed area.
  - Drag the slider to the left or right to zoom in or out.
- Choose **Save when you are done.**

What is iCloud?

iCloud facilitates the safe, current, and universal access of your most critical data, including backups, files, and images. Sharing documents, notes, images, and more with friends and family is also made simple with iCloud. You may get a free email account and 5 GB of free data storage with iCloud. You can upgrade to iCloud+ for more features and storage. To begin configuring iCloud on your Mac, log in with your Apple ID. Important iCloud services, such as iCloud Drive, iCloud Photos, and more, are configured immediately when you log in. You have complete control over the settings for each of your devices and may switch these features on or off whenever you want. **Here are a few methods for using iCloud on a Mac.**

iCloud feature	Description
Photos icon	Every single picture and video you have. Constantly accessible. Your images and videos are safely stored by iCloud Photos, which also allows you to access them online at iCloud.com and across all of your devices. Sharing pictures and videos with the individuals you choose is simple with shared albums, which also allow you to invite others to contribute pictures, videos, and comments. Study up on Pictures. You may work together with up to five family members or friends on a shared photo and video library with iCloud Shared Photo Library, allowing you to cherish more comprehensive memories in one location.

iCloud Drive icon	Store all of your files safely on iCloud Drive. iCloud Drive allows you to manage and safely save your files. Access and maintain them on iCloud.com and across all of your devices. To make your Mac Desktop and Documents folders accessible from anywhere, you may also add them to iCloud Drive. You can work together on and exchange files that are stored in iCloud. You control who has access to your content and may edit it. Everyone sees changes made by participants to the content instantly.
Family Sharing icon	Give your family access to music, books, apps, subscriptions, and more. You can share access to incredible Apple services like Apple Music, Apple TV+, iCloud+, Apple Fitness+, Apple News+, and Apple Arcade with up to five other family members thanks to Family Sharing. A family photo album, an iCloud storage plan, and purchases made through iTunes, Apple Books, and the App Store can all be shared by your group. You can even assist in finding each other's misplaced electronics. You may share all of the iCloud+ features and included storage with your family members when you have an iCloud+ subscription.
iCloud Private Relay icon	Protect your unencrypted internet traffic and hide your IP address and browsing behavior in Safari to ensure that no one, not even Apple, can know who you are or what websites you visit. accessible with iCloud+
Hide My Email icon	By generating distinct, arbitrary email addresses that are forwarded to your inbox and may be deleted at any time, you can keep your personal email address private. Accessible via iCloud+.
Safari	Tab Groups, Reading List, open tabs, and Safari bookmarks

Even when you're not online, you can read articles from your |

	Reading List, synchronize your open browser tabs across all of your devices, and access the same bookmarks. Additionally, work on Tab Groups with others and make sure your Tab Groups are current across all of your devices.
iCloud storage	Everyone begins with a free 5 GB iCloud storage plan, and upgrading is simple and available whenever needed. Your iCloud storage space is only required for files, backups of your devices, images, videos, and apps; it is not used for purchases made from the iTunes Store or apps. iCloud data is secured, and two-factor verification limits account access to reliable devices only.

What is iCloud+?

All of iCloud's features are included in iCloud+, along with additional premium features including support for custom email domains, iCloud Private Relay, Hide My Email, HomeKit Secure Video, and all the storage you require for your data.

Subscribe to iCloud+

Both iCloud+ and Apple One, which combines iCloud+ with additional services, are available for subscription. Take note: Not all nations or areas may have access to iCloud+.

Share iCloud+

You can distribute your iCloud+ subscription to other members of your Family Sharing group after setting up Family Sharing. If you already have an iCloud+ or Apple One membership and you join a Family Sharing group that has one as well, you use the group's subscription rather than having your own renewed on your next billing date. A Family Sharing group that you join that isn't subscribed will make use of your subscription. You can cancel your Family Sharing subscription, quit the group, or stop utilizing Family Sharing to stop sharing iCloud+.

Change or cancel your iCloud+ subscription

The same process you use to adjust your iCloud storage plan can also be used to modify or terminate your iCloud+ subscription.

Store files in iCloud Drive

You may securely save any form of document in iCloud with iCloud Drive, and you can view it from any device or online at iCloud.com. Mac computers running OS X 10.10 or later, iOS devices running iOS 8 or later, iPadOS devices, and Windows PCs running iCloud for Windows (Windows 7 or later required) can all use iCloud Drive. All of your devices need to have the same Apple ID registered on them and have the minimum system requirements met. It should be noted that files and data on your devices that do not have iCloud Drive enabled are not synced with files and data on your devices that do.

Set up iCloud Drive

You can configure iCloud Drive on this Mac right now in the iCloud settings if you haven't already.

- Select **System Settings from the Apple menu on your Mac**, and then select [your name] in the sidebar's upper section. If your name is not displayed, select "**Sign in with your Apple ID**," type in your password, your Apple ID, and any Reachable At email addresses or phone numbers you may have added in the Apple ID settings. You can create an Apple ID if you don't already have one.
- Toggle on Sync this Mac by selecting iCloud from the menu on the right, then iCloud Drive.
- Select **Done**.

Store your Desktop and Documents folders in iCloud Drive

You may set up iCloud Drive to automatically store all of the files in your Documents and Desktop folders. In this manner, files are saved exactly where you typically put them and are accessible from all of your devices as well as iCloud.com.

- Select **System Settings from the Apple menu on your Mac**, and then select [your name] in the sidebar's upper section. If your name is not displayed, select "**Sign in with your Apple ID**," type in your password, your Apple ID, and any Reachable At email addresses or phone numbers you may have added in the Apple ID settings. You can create an Apple ID if you don't already have one.
- Ensure that iCloud Drive is switched on by clicking iCloud Drive after selecting iCloud on the right.

- Activate the **Documents & Desktop Folders.**
- Press "**Done.**"

Your Desktop and Documents folders are transferred to iCloud Drive after you enable Desktop & Documents Folders. They also show up in the Files app on your iPhone or iPad, as well as in the iCloud part of the Finder sidebar on your Mac. On your Mac, you can easily see the iCloud Drive's sync status. Point and select the status or information icon on iCloud Drive in the Finder sidebar.

Share and collaborate on files and folders

To work together on projects, you can share folders and files using iCloud Drive with other people. The individuals you invite can view and, depending on the permissions you select, collaborate on the shared objects after downloading them from iCloud to any of their devices. The next time you access the files on your Mac, you can view any updates.

Note: You must have macOS 10.15.4 or later, iOS 13.4 or later, or iCloud for Windows version 11.1 or later on your computer or device to use iCloud Drive folder sharing.

Invite people to collaborate on files or folders

- **On your Mac, perform one of the following to ask others to work together on files or folders:**
    - After opening a Finder window by clicking the Dock's Finder icon, choose a file or folder from the sidebar by clicking **iCloud Drive, and then hit the Share button.**
    - To share an object on the desktop, control-click **it and select it from the shortcut menu.**

Note: A file or folder needs to be in iCloud Drive for others to work on it with you.

- Choose **Collaborate from the menu that pops up.**
- To set permissions for collaboration, click "**Only invited people can edit.**" below "**Collaborate.**" Next, select an option from the pop-up menu below "Who can access":
    - Only those who have been invited: Only those you invite should be able to access the file or folder.
    - Anyone in possession of the link: Permit access to the file or folder to anybody who receives the link. If you select this option, the individuals you invite may forward the link and grant access to those who were not on your initial invitation list.

- Select a choice from the following options when the pop-up menu appears beneath Permissions:
  - Able to modify: Permit the individuals you invite to read and edit the file or folder's contents.
  - View only: Permit guests to access the file or folder's contents, but not edit them.
- To enable sharing of the file or folder with other people, tick the box next to **"Allow others to invite."** To limit who can share the file or folder with others, deselect the checkbox.
- Create and copy a link to the shared item, or share the invitation using Mail or Messages.

The shared file or folder can be downloaded from iCloud to any of the devices of the individuals you invite once they accept your invitation. If you permit them, they can edit a file, and the next time you open it on your Mac, you'll see the changes. Only the individuals you have invited can access the files in a shared folder that you have shared. You cannot alter the settings of a single file inside the folder; instead, you must adjust the shared folder's parameters to add more participants. Control-click the file or folder in the Finder or on the desktop, select Share from the shortcut menu, select Send Copy from the pop-up menu, and then select the method you want to use to share the copy of the item—such as AirDrop or Mail—if you want to send it without working together on it.

Accept an invitation to a shared file or folder

To view the shared item in the Finder and add it to iCloud Drive on your Mac, select the link you received, then select Open. **A shared file or folder becomes available in the following locations once you accept an invitation to access it:**
- On your Mac, in iCloud Drive
- The Files app (iOS 11 or later) on your iOS or iPadOS device
- On iCloud.com
- On a Windows computer running iCloud

If you have authorization to edit, you can open the shared object in any compatible app and make changes. The most recent updates are visible to all users who have access to the item when they open it again.

Manage iCloud storage

You instantly get 5 GB of free storage when you activate iCloud and log in with your Apple ID. You can store files, backups, images, and more on your iCloud storage. Upgrading to iCloud+ will boost your storage capacity. View Describe iCloud+.

To free up more space in iCloud, you can also delete things that are saved there.

- Select **System Settings** from the Apple menu on your Mac, then **click [your name] in the sidebar's upper section. If your name is not displayed, select "Sign in with your Apple ID,"** type in your password, your Apple ID, and any Reachable At email addresses or phone numbers you may have added in the Apple ID settings. You can create an Apple ID if you don't already have one.
- To perform any of the following actions, select iCloud on the right, then click **Manage**:
  - Get your storage upgraded: After selecting **Modify Storage Plan or Add Storage, adhere to the on-screen directions.**
  - Share iCloud+ with your family: Click **Share with Family** after subscribing to iCloud+, then adhere to the prompts on the screen. You can distribute iCloud+ with your loved ones using the Family Sharing option if Share with Family isn't shown.

    Note: The storage increase is charged to the family organizer's account if you use the same Apple ID for purchases made as a family and you're part of a Family Sharing group.
- Examine how a feature or program uses storage: On an app or feature in the list, click it. For an app, you can permanently delete all of its data and documents. Document copies can be saved before being deleted from iCloud.
- Take out a backup of an iOS or iPadOS device: Choose a device whose backup you don't require by clicking **Backups in the list, and then click Remove (below the backup list).** WARNING: iCloud will no longer automatically backup your current iOS or iPadOS device if you remove the backup.
- Switch off **Siri and erase any data connected to it**: From the list, select **Siri,** then select Disable and Delete.

- Choose **Done**.

Activity

- Manage Apple ID settings and configure your Apple ID picture.
- What exactly is iCloud+?
- Set up iCloud drive and store files in iCloud drive.
- Effectively manage your iCloud storage.

CHAPTER 12

FAMILY AND FRIENDS

What is Family Sharing?

You may share subscriptions to Apple services like Apple Music, Apple TV+, iCloud+, Apple Fitness+, Apple News+, and Apple Arcade with up to five other family members with Family Sharing. A family photo album, an iCloud storage plan, and purchases made through the iTunes Store, App Store, and Apple Books can all be shared by your family group. You can even assist in finding each other's misplaced electronics. Up to five family members can be invited to join Family Sharing, which is set up by one adult who acts as the family organizer.

This adult also selects which features the family can enjoy. Family members can access the shared content immediately upon joining. To access Family settings, each member of the family must have an Apple ID and be signed in with it. A child can be added to the group and have an Apple ID created for them by the organizer, a parent, or a guardian. Note: one family (adults and children) is the intended user base for Family Sharing. One Family Sharing group is all that you can be a part of at once. Mac computers running OS X 10.10 or later, iOS devices running iOS 8 or later, iPadOS devices, and Windows PCs using iCloud for Windows (Windows 7 or later required) can all use Family Sharing.

Set up Family Sharing

Family members are invited to join the Family Sharing group by one adult, who acts as the family organizer. **For each family member to join the group, they must have an Apple ID.**

- Select **System Settings** from the Apple menu on your Mac, and then select [your name] in the sidebar's upper section. If your name is not displayed, select **"Sign in with your Apple ID,"** type in your password, your Apple ID, and any Reachable At email addresses or phone numbers you may have added in the Apple ID settings. You can create an Apple ID if you don't already have one.
- Invite individuals to join your Family Sharing group by clicking the **Family Sharing button on the right followed by Set Up Family**:

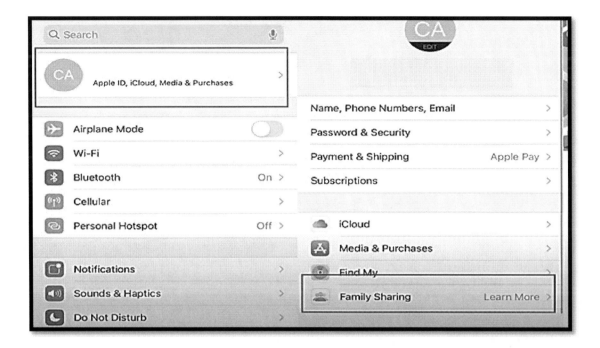

- Include your family: Click **Invite People** then adhere to the directions displayed on the screen. To extend an invitation to someone in person, select Invite in Person and request that they sign in to your Mac with their Apple ID and password. If not, Mail, Messages, or AirDrop can be used to send the invitation. You cannot accept an invitation sent to someone who does not already have an Apple ID; they must create one.
- Make a younger child's Apple ID: After clicking "**Create Child Account,**" adhere to the on-screen directions.
- To expand your Family Sharing group with more family members, select **Add Member and adhere to the prompts displayed on the screen.**

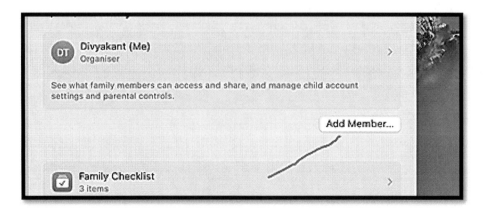

- Take one of the following actions:

- ○ **Finish the suggested tasks**: Select the **Family Checklist option**. A list of recommendations appears to help you make the most of Family Sharing. You can add a recovery contact, reveal your location, and set up parental controls for children, for instance.
- ○ **Look for shared subscription services to use:** Select **Subscriptions.** A list of your subscribed services that you can share is displayed. To share with your family, click the subscription name and then adhere to the on-screen directions. All of your family's Apple subscriptions are automatically shared, except iCloud+. Family members have the option of maintaining their separate storage plans or you can decide to share iCloud+. Choose Apple Subscriptions or the service name below Discover More to see more about the other Apple subscriptions available. Select **Discover next to Subscriptions for Family in the App Store to view additional family subscriptions.**
- ○ **Construct a purchase sharing system**: Click **Buy Sharing, then select Turn On Purchase Sharing after clicking Proceed.** All members of your family can access purchases made through the iTunes Store, App Store, and Apple Books by sharing them. Every purchase is performed using the shared payment method that you configured.
- ○ Configure location sharing by clicking Location Sharing and turning it on for yourself and any member of your family who you wish to share your whereabouts with. To automatically share your location with any future family members who join, turn on Automatically Share Location. It is possible to configure location sharing so that users of the Messages and Find My applications can see each other's whereabouts. The Find My app is available for usage on Mac, iOS, and iPadOS devices.
- ○ **Configure Ask to Buy:** Click the name of a child in your Family Sharing group, select **Ask To Buy from the sidebar, and then select Turn On Ask to Buy to set up Ask to**

Buy. With this configuration, kids in your Family Sharing group must ask your permission before downloading or making purchases from the iTunes Store, Apple Books, or the App Store. Ask to Buy age limitations differ by location. In the US, Ask to Buy can be enabled for any family member under the age of 18, and it is enabled by default for kids under the age of 13.

    ○ **Put parental limits and screen time in place**: After selecting the desired options, click **the family member's name, click Screen Time in the sidebar, and then click Open [family member's] Screen Time**. Age limitations on screen time differ by location. For every family member under the age of 18, the family organizer in the US can activate Screen Time.

Set up Screen Time for a child

Using family sharing to set up and monitor a child's screen time is the most adaptable and practical method. With Family Sharing, you can use any Mac, iPhone, or iPad to remotely control and keep an eye on each child's device usage from your account. You can still set up Screen Time for a youngster by connecting to their Mac account even if you aren't using Family Sharing.

Note: The Web Content Filter limits adult content for children under 13, and Communication Safety and Screen Distance are on by default.

- **Try one of the following suggestions on your Mac:**
  - ○ Make sure you are signed in with your Apple ID when you log into your Mac user account if you are using Family Sharing.
  - ○ Enter the child's Mac user account to log in if you are not using Family Sharing.
- Select **System Settings from the Apple menu, and then select Screen Time from the sidebar. (You might have to scroll below.)**
- Select **a child by clicking the pop-up menu on the right if you are using Family Sharing.**
- Choose **Set up Screen Time for Your Child, select Turn on Screen Time, and then adhere to the prompts displayed on the screen.** You can establish time away from displays, set content limitations, enable Screen Distance, enable App & Website Activity, and generate a 4-digit Screen Time passcode during the setup process.
- **Scroll down to the Screen Time settings and activate any of the following:**
  - ○ Include Website Data: Select this option to enable the inclusion of specific website visitation information in Screen Time reports. In the absence of this setting, webpages are simply recorded as Safari usage.

○ Enable the **"Lock Screen Time Settings" option** to extend the time after limits expire and make Screen Time settings require a passcode. Note: You are requested to change the family member's administrator account to a regular account if they have one.

Share purchases with your family

If you're a part of a Family Sharing group, purchases made by other group members are instantly available to you. On your Mac, iOS device, or iPadOS device, you can download their purchases whenever you like. Your purchases are accessible to other group members in the same manner. You can keep specific purchases private if you don't want other group members to know about them. Purchase sharing can only be set up by the family organizer (see Set up Family Sharing).

View and download purchases made by other family members

Depending on the app, there are differences in how you download purchases made by other family members.

- Listen to or download music: Open the Mac version of the Music app, log in, and select **Account > Purchased**. Select a family member by **clicking the pop-up menu next to Purchased, and then download the desired things.**
- To view or download apps, log in to your Mac's App Store and select Store > Account. Select a family member by clicking the **"Purchased by" pop-up option, and then download the desired items.**
- To hide books, log in to your Mac's Books program and select **All (or another collection) from the sidebar. To conceal an item, click the More Options icon below it, select Remove, and then select Conceal.**

Stop sharing your purchases

Your family members will no longer be able to access any purchases you make jointly from the iTunes Store, App Store, and Apple Books.

- Select **System Settings** from the Apple menu on your Mac, and then select **Family** from the sidebar. If Family is not visible, enable Family Sharing.
- Toggle off **Share My Purchases** by clicking [your name] after selecting Purchase Sharing on the right.

Turn off purchase sharing

Your family members will no longer be able to make new shared purchases from the iTunes Store, App Store, or Apple Books if you disable purchase sharing for your Family Sharing group.

The only person who may disable purchase sharing for the group is the family organizer.

- Select **System Settings** from the Apple menu on your Mac, then select **Family from the sidebar. If Family is not visible, enable Family Sharing.**
- On the right, select **Purchase Sharing**. Next, select **Stop Purchase Sharing**. Finally, select Stop Purchase Sharing once more.

Watch and listen together with SharePlay

You may utilize SharePlay in FaceTime with macOS 12 or later to include TV episodes, movies, and music in your video calls. You may have a real-time connection with every caller thanks to shared controls and simultaneous playback, which allows you to all see and hear the same moments at the same time. Smart volume allows you to watch or listen while chatting because it automatically adjusts the audio.

Note: To participate in SharePlay, some apps need to be subscribed to. Not every country or area has access to every feature or piece of information.

Watch video together

When having a FaceTime call with someone else, you can watch movies and TV series. Everyone on the call can watch the same moments at the same time and use the shared playback controls to hit Play or Pause if they all have access to the video content (for example, through a subscription or free trial). The volume of the movie or show automatically adjusts so you may continue conversing while watching. Start viewing a film or television program on the Apple TV app while you're on a FaceTime chat on your Mac.

- Verify that you wish to use SharePlay if this is your first time using it. SharePlay launches automatically after that. You will be prompted the next time you wish to utilize the Apple TV app's SharePlay feature if you choose to **start Only for Me**.

All call participants with content access can view simultaneously. Those without access are urged to obtain it (either by payment, subscription or, if offered, a free trial). Everyone may utilize the playback controls on their individual Apple devices to fast-forward, rewind, pause, or play in real-time while they're all watching together.

Listen to music together

You can arrange a FaceTime call with other people to listen to music together. If all participants in the call have the necessary access to the music, they can all hear the song simultaneously, see the title and the next song, and utilize the shared controls to pause, reorder, add to the queue, and advance to the next track. It automatically adjusts the music volume so you can converse while listening.

- To begin listening to music on your Mac while on a FaceTime chat, move your pointer over any song or album in the Music app and click the **Play button.**

Verify that you wish to use SharePlay if this is your first time using it. SharePlay launches automatically after that. You will be prompted the next time you wish to utilize **SharePlay for Music if you choose to start Only for Me**. At the same moment, the music begins to play for every caller with access to the material. Those without access are urged to obtain it (either by payment, subscription or, if offered, a free trial).

- Anybody on the call can oversee the shared Playing Next queue, examine lyrics, and control playback while everyone is listening together (including pausing the music, skipping to the next song, and more).

Share a Photo Library

You can work together with up to five family members or friends on a photo collection with iCloud Shared Photo Library, allowing you to cherish more comprehensive memories in one location. One Shared Library membership is allowed at a time. Every member of the Shared Library can see, modify, and remove the images and videos you contribute when you create or join one. They remain in your Library. Family members or friends who own an iPhone or iPad running iOS 16 or iPadOS 16 and can access iCloud Shared Photo Library can also be invited. Mac users must have macOS 13 or later. To participate, users must have activated iCloud Photos on their Mac or other devices and have an Apple ID. Children under 13 must be enrolled in the iCloud Family Sharing group created by the organizer. The Shared Library is available to users on iCloud.com, Mac, iPhone, iPad, Apple TV, and PC.

Set up a shared Library

- Select **Photos > Settings, click Shared Library**, and then click **Get Started from within the Photos app on your Mac.**

- To invite a family member or friend to join the shared library, select the **Add Object button**, pick the person by clicking their name, and then click **Add**. This process can be repeated to invite a maximum of five people.

- Press the **Next button.**
- Select one of the following to push photos to the shared library:
  - **All My Photos and Videos**: Transfer all of your current images and movies to the shared library. After selecting Next, adhere to the on-screen directions. Note: Nothing is sent to the Shared Library about screenshots, screen captures, or hidden things.
  - **Sort Pictures and Videos by People or Date**: Organize pictures and videos that feature particular people or were shot after a particular date. After selecting people, click the **Add Object button and click Next**. Then, click **Add Other People.** To add photographs by date, click **Skip.** To select the start date for the photographs you want to be included, follow the on-screen directions.
- To view the contents of the Shared Library, select **Preview Shared Library**; alternatively, select **Skip**. Click **Proceed** once the Shared Library has been viewed.
- To send text invitations to participants, click **Invite via Messages.** Alternatively, click **Copy Link to insert the link into an email that can be sent to attendees.**
- Press "**Done.**"

The Photos window displays your newly created shared library. When the Library pop-up menu shows up in the toolbar, you can select to access your Personal Library, the Shared Library, or both libraries simultaneously.

Join a Shared Library

You can view, edit, add, favorite, caption, and remove items from a shared library once you accept an invitation to join it.

- Click the **Shared Library Invitation link in the email or text message invitation**, then adhere to the on-screen directions. You can contribute your images to the Shared Library once you accept the invitation.

Add or Remove Shared Library Participants

You can add and delete participants from a shared library if you are the organizer.

- Select **Photos** > **Settings** from within the Photos app on your Mac, and then select **Shared Library**.
- Take one of the following actions:
  - **Add participants**: To include a family member or friend with an Apple ID, click **Add Participants**, type their name, click to **pick it, and then click Add.**
    An email requesting them to join the Shared Library is sent to the people you add. To add up to five persons, repeat this process. Click the **More icon next to the person you've added, select Resend Invitation, and then send the invitation again.**
- **Remove participants:** To remove someone, click the **More button next to their name, select Remove, and then select Remove from Shared Library.** Individuals you delete get notified and have the option to transfer every item from the Shared Library to their Library. (If someone is removed from the Shared Library before they have had seven days to join, they will only be able to access the materials they have contributed.)

Leave or delete a Shared Library

Anytime they want, users of a shared library are free to depart. You can remove a Shared Library if you are its organizer. Everyone involved gets notified when the Shared Library is deleted, and they can decide to save every item from the Shared Library in their Library. You are only allowed to retain the materials you have contributed to a shared library if you depart from it within 7 days of joining.

- Select **Photos** > **Settings** from within the Photos app on your Mac, and then select **Shared Library**.
- If you are the organizer or a participant, select **Delete Shared Library or Leave Shared Library, respectively.**
- Choose one of the subsequent choices:
  - Keep everything: Include every image from the Public Library in your collection.
  - Keep only what I contributed: To your Library, only add images that you have added to the Shared Library.
- Press **Delete Library to remove it.**
- To verify the deletion, select **Delete Shared Library once more.**

Collaborate on projects

In Messages, you can extend an invitation to work together on a project, and all participants are immediately added to the document, spreadsheet, or other shared file. You can see activity updates at the top of the Messages chat when someone adjusts. To return to the shared material, click the updates. Note: Before you and your recipients may begin working together on a project using Messages, you must save the content in a location that can be accessible by others, like iCloud Drive, and use iMessage on macOS 13 or later, iOS 16 or later, or iPadOS 16.1 or later. Before you can work together on macOS apps, you must enable each app's iCloud functionality.

Drag a file into a Message conversation to start collaborating

You may instantly add files and folders from iCloud Drive, Keynote, Numbers, and Pages into individual or group conversations when you want to work together.
- Drag a file or folder to be shared to a discussion in the Messages app from the Finder or your Mac's desktop.
- **Enter one of the following in the field located at the bottom of the Message conversation:**
    ○ If the option isn't already selected, click the pop-up menu and select **Collaborate.**
    ○ To modify the sharing options, click **the arrow beneath the pop-up menu.**
- Choose **Return** to transmit the message.

Updates are displayed at the top of the Message conversation whenever someone makes changes to the file. Click an update to see the changes and go back to the shared project.

Manage a project in Messages

In the Mac Messages program, once you share a project in a private or public conversation, you can execute any of the following:
- **Go to a project:** Select the shared project link in the discussion. Alternatively, select the shared project by clicking the Info button located in the upper-right corner of a chat, then scrolling to Collaboration.
- **See the project modifications and who made them.** When someone makes an edit, go to the top of the conversation and choose **Show or Review.**
- **Add a person to a project:** When you're working on a project with a group, you can add people to the group conversation in the same manner you normally would. Then grant them access to the project by clicking **Review at the top of the transcript.**

- **Remove a person from a project**: If you're working on a project with a group, you can exclude someone from the group conversation in the same manner you normally would. Then, check the participant's access to the app (such as Notes or Pages) to remove reading or editing privileges.
- **Pin a project.** In the chat, Control-click the shared project and select **Pin**.
- Hide a project by clicking the **Info button** in the top-right corner of the discussion, scrolling to Collaboration, and then Control-clicking the shared project and selecting Hide. When you conceal a project, it no longer displays below Collaboration (but still appears in the Links section). Hiding a project does not revoke your sharing access or remove you from the collaboration. You continue to access the project through the app in which it was shared.
- Share a project by clicking **the Info button** in the top-right corner of a discussion, scrolling to Collaboration, and then Control-clicking the shared project and selecting Share.

Play games with your friends

On your Mac, you can play games in single-player or multiplayer modes. If you don't already have one, a Game Center account is set up for you when you log in with your Apple ID. To get the newest or most well-liked titles that utilize Game Center, you can peruse the Mac App Store. Many iPhone and iPad games are compatible with Macs running Apple hardware; these titles can be identified in the App Store by looking for the Designed for iPhone or Designed for iPad logo. To download and play a variety of innovative games on all of your compatible devices, you may also subscribe to Apple Arcade. Note: Not all nations or areas have access to the Apple Arcade or Game Center services.

Customize your Game Center account

- Select **System Settings** from the Apple menu on your Mac, then pick **Game Center from** the sidebar. (You might have to scroll below.)
  - **Take one of the following actions:**
  - ○ **Modify your nickname**: After entering a new moniker (which serves as your gamer ID), hit **Return**.
  - ○ **Modify who has access to your profile**: Select Who Can See Your Profile in Games by clicking **the pop-up menu next to Profile Privacy and selecting either Everyone, Friends only, or Just You.** Your achievements and the games you've been playing are displayed on your profile. All other players can always see your avatar and Game Center moniker.

○ **Enable friends to locate you:** Activate **Allow Locating by Friends** so that friends can locate you using the name they have on file in the Contacts app's contacts list.

○ **Accept requests exclusively from contacts.** To ensure that the only friend requests you receive come from your connections, turn on Requests from Connections Only.

○ Let players that are close to you invite you to play a multiplayer game: Activate the Nearby Players. Turn it off if you don't want to be discovered. Players who are nearby are those who are within Bluetooth® range or on the same Wi-Fi network as you.

○ **Connect with friends:** Enable the feature that lets you connect to others in your friends list while playing games. You can stop sharing your friends list with apps if you don't want games to connect to your pals.

○ **Invite friends:** To send invitations using the Messages app, choose **Invite Friends.**

○ **Friend addition or removal:** To view your Game Center profile on the App Store, select **Show Profile.**

Use a game controller

Playing games on your Mac is possible with a gaming controller connected. If your game controller allows it, you can set up events to happen on your Mac when you press specific buttons on the controller. Some examples of these events include opening the Games folder in Launchpad, taking a screenshot, or recording a quick gameplay video.

- When your gaming controller is connected to your Mac, select **System Settings from the Apple menu, then select Gaming Controller from the sidebar to adjust these settings.**

Play multiplayer games

Note: To play certain games, compatible hardware and software are needed.
- **Allow a game to find other players**: If the game has Auto-match, click **Play Now to let it search for other players for you.**
- **Play nearby players:** If the game detects players who are on the same Wi-Fi network as you or within Bluetooth range, it will display them. In the game, choose a player.
- **Ask friends to play:** In the game, select **Invite Friends, then choose from your contacts, friends, or nearby players.** Customize your invitation if desired, then click Send. You might send your invitation as a message or via SMS to a specific phone number.
- Accept the invitation: In a notification or message, select **Accept.** The game launches (if you have it) and you may begin playing. If you don't already have the game, the App Store will open so you can get it.
- **Capture a short video or take a screenshot while playing**: When using a Bluetooth game controller that has support for it, press and hold the game controller button

you've designated for recording or taking screenshots. You can record a maximum of 15 seconds of gameplay.

To receive notifications when you are requested to join a game or when it is your turn to play, make sure that Game Center notifications are enabled in the Notifications settings. Notifications from Game Center are still accessible while you're using a Focus. To reduce screen stutters, input lag, and screen tearing while playing games on a Mac connected to an adaptive sync display, you can enable an option that automatically modifies the display's refresh rate to match the frame rate output by the graphics processing unit (GPU).

Activity

- Configure family sharing on your Mac.
- Download music and listen with your family with the use of SharePlay.
- Set up a shared library and share a photo library with your family and friends.
- Play games with your friends.

CHAPTER 13

LISTEN, WATCH, AND READ

Play Music

You can personalize how you listen to your music by adjusting the sequence in which songs play, repeating tracks, and more using the options in the Music window.

- To locate music in your music collection using the Mac's Music program, try any of the following:
  - Locate a particular song or album: Select any item from the sidebar below the Library. For instance, to see every album in your library, click **Albums**.
  - Select a playlist: From the sidebar, select **a playlist by clicking on it.**
  - Look through your music collection.
- Select a song or album by moving the pointer over it, and then press the **Play button.**
- Additionally, you can filter the music, queue them up in a particular sequence, shuffle and repeat them, and stop a song from playing. A CD can be used to listen to music.

Listen to podcasts

You can play the entire podcast or just certain episodes when you find one you want to listen to.

- On your Mac, select **any item in the sidebar of the Podcasts app.**
- Click the **Play button** after moving the pointer over the show or episode you want to watch. The show art and playback controls display at the top of the podcast window when the episode starts playing. Certain shows have original artwork that is displayed on the episode page and in the player for each episode.
- With the use of the playback controls get any of the following done:
  - Press the **Play or Pause button located in the center,** or utilize the Touch Bar's playback controls. Moreover, you may play, pause, and continue an episode by using the Spacebar.
  - To advance or rewind an episode, click the **Skip Forward or Backward buttons,** which will advance the playback in 30-second intervals. Alternatively, you can use the Touch Bar's playback controls.
  - **Rewind or fast-forward**: Drag the progress handle to the left to rewind or to the right to fast-forward, or click a point on the progress bar to jump straight to that spot. (Alternatively, you can utilize the Touch Bar's playback controls.)

- Modify the speed of the playback: After selecting **Controls > Playback Speed, select a speed.**
- **Adjust volume**: To change the volume, drag the volume slider to the right or left (or use the Touch Bar's playback controls).
- Handle the episode (copying the URL, sharing the episode, or visiting the Show page, for instance): Move the cursor over the currently playing episode, select an option, and then click the **More button.**
- Examine the description of the episode: Press the **"Episode Notes" icon**. Until you click the Episode Notes button once more to close it, the episode description remains visible on the screen.

Watch TV shows and movies

If you have an MLS Season Pass, you may watch Major League Soccer matches in addition to movies, TV series, and Friday Night Baseball from Home in the Apple TV app (note that not all programming is available in all countries or regions). Choose what you want to watch, bookmark it for later, or just dive right in.

Browse content

- On your Mac, open the Apple TV app.
- Using the sidebar, select Home. You can see items you've added to Up Next, including videos you've started but not yet finished, in the Up Next row.
- View suggested TV series, films, and events by scrolling down. Expert-selected collections and categories based on your viewing preferences are also available.
- To view an item's rating, description, available channels, and details about how to buy or rent it, click on it.

When you click on an Apple TV channel in the channel's row, the channel's main page loads. From there, you may subscribe, see TV series, movies, and events by scrolling down, and then click on an item.

Browse channels

- On your Mac, open **the Apple TV app.**
- Using the sidebar, select **Home.**
- To view every channel you currently subscribe to or discover new ones, scroll down to the channel's row and then go right. Note: The sidebar also shows channels that you have subscriptions to.
- To open an item, click on it.

See what's up next

Content that you have already started watching or want to watch is shown in the Up Next row.

- To view shows you've recently watched or added to Up Next, select **Home from the sidebar of the Apple TV app on your Mac, scroll to the Up Next row, and then move left or right.**

In the order that you are most likely to want to watch them, shows and movies are presented. For instance, Up Next automatically updates with the next TV show after one is done. Additionally, if you've already caught up on a show, a new episode always shows up at the top of the Up Next row as soon as it's available. Your watching history and episode selection in the Apple TV app on your iPhone, iPad, iPod touch, or Apple TV remain synchronized if you are logged in with the same Apple ID that you use on your Mac. For instance, you can begin viewing a show on your Mac and complete it on your iPad, or the other way around.

Play a movie, TV show, or sports event

- Select **Home in the sidebar of the Apple TV app on your Mac**, then select an item from the right.
- **Take one of the following actions:**
  - Play the object: Press the **Play button.** (You can use the Play button to access content on Apple TV channels you subscribe to, as well as content that is free or that you have already bought or rented.)
  - To become an Apple TV+ subscriber, click the **subscription button and then adhere to the on-screen directions.**
  - Get an Apple TV channel subscription: After selecting the subscription option, adhere to the on-screen directions.
  - To purchase or rent a movie, click the **Buy or Rent button,** choose your preferred choice, and complete the transaction.

Read and listen to books

After you obtain books from the bookstore or install books you bought on other devices, you can begin reading and appreciating them. If you'd prefer to have a book read to you, you could like listening to audiobooks.

Open and move around in a book

- Double-click a book to open it in the Books app on your Mac by selecting Books (or another collection) from the sidebar. Note: Double-clicking the book will download it from iCloud if it has an iCloud status icon beneath it (you may need to log in first).
- Turn the pages of the book:
  - **Refer to the contents table:** Point **the cursor to the top of the book,** then, depending on the book, click **either the Thumbnails or the Table of Contents button.**
  - **Navigate to the previous or next page:** To select the arrow that appears, drag **the pointer to the left or right edge of the book.**
  - You can also utilize the Touch Bar, the arrow keys on the keyboard, or swipe right or left across a trackpad or Magic Mouse.
  - Navigate **to the top of the book, s**elect the **magnifying glass,** then type a **word, phrase, or page number to start a search**. Another option is to pick some text, Control-click it, and select Search.
  - **View the page you were just on:** After making a multipage jump, click the Back icon in the lower-left corner of the page. When browsing search results or different portions of the book's table of contents, this is helpful.
  - Click the **Return icon** in the bottom-right corner of the page to go back to the page you were on before.

See what you are currently reading

On your Mac, select Home from the sidebar of the Books app. The books you are reading right now are listed in Continue.

- To view a list of books you've bought, click **All in the sidebar under Library if you haven't begun reading any yet.**

Drag the pointer over the title of a book or audiobook in Home, select Remove from the menu, and then make your selection.

Save your place with a bookmark

- Double-click a book to open it in the Books app on your Mac by selecting Books (or another collection) from the sidebar.
- Place the pointer at the top of the page you wish to bookmark, and then tap the Bookmark button (or utilize the Touch Bar).

The Bookmark icon is solid if you already have a bookmark on the page. Select the Show Bookmarks icon to view every bookmark in the book. **Click on the Bookmark icon to delete a bookmark.**

Have a book read to you

- Double-click a book to open it in the Books app on your Mac by selecting Books (or another collection) from the sidebar.
- **Take one of the subsequent actions:**
  - When reading a book that has the Read Aloud function enabled, utilize the Touch Bar or the Play button located in the toolbar at the top of the book. Select **a page-turning option by clicking the pop-up menu that appears next to the Play button.**
  - Regarding any book: Navigate to the desired page and select **Edit > Speech > Begin Speaking.**

Translate text in a book

- Choose the text you wish to translate in the MacBook app.
- Select Translate [selection] by controlling-clicking the selection. (This content cannot be translated into Books if you do not see this option.)
- After selecting the source language, select the **target language for translation.**

Read the news

Apple News gathers and arranges news from a variety of sources (referred to as channels) and subjects. It's simple to browse around and locate the content and sources that pique your interest, whether it's summer food ideas, trip videos, or breaking news.

- Click an item in the sidebar of the News app on your Mac. If the sidebar isn't visible, select the Sidebar icon in the toolbar. The sidebar offers quick access to stories you've saved and your reading history.
  - This displays the best news that Apple News editors have chosen, together with stories from the channels and subjects you are interested in. The Today stream, which features curated and customized local stories and weather forecasts based on your location, may contain local news in select nations or regions. The Today stream also features My Publications, which displays issues from publications you follow, if you have an Apple News+ subscription.
  - News+, which displays hundreds of periodicals, widely read newspapers, and additional sources that are accessible through Apple News+. You can explore recent issues, download issues, select a publication to read, and do a lot more if you're a subscriber. You can look through publications and headlines if you haven't subscribed yet.

- Sports, where you can view highlights, get stories from major sports publications, local newspapers, and more; follow your favorite teams, leagues, athletes, and sports; and get scores, schedules, and standings for the best professional and collegiate leagues.
- Puzzles: Daily crossword, crossword mini, and Quartiles puzzles are available for Apple News+ users to solve.
- Shared with You allows you to easily locate and read tales that other users have shared with you through the Messages app in one convenient spot.
- You can only have a certain number of Favorites. Favorites display the channels and topics that you find most appealing from your Following list. Though you can edit your list at any moment, there may already be some channels and subjects that are automatically added to your Favorites.
- The channels and subjects you follow are listed below. Apple News Spotlight is another feature in this section that features content chosen by Apple News editors and coverage of noteworthy events.

- Explore the News+ feed or stories on the right. Stories from channels you've blocked appear with a gray title and a notification letting you know that you've blocked the channel when you explore Top Stories and other sections that showcase stories hand-picked by Apple News editors.
- To read an article, click on it. To explore issues and stories, click **on a publication in the News+ feed. You have a choice of what to do while reading a story**:
  - Watch videos, request that more or fewer stories similar to it be shown, share it with others, or save it for later reading.
  - Use the Left or Right Arrow keys to navigate to the previous or next tale.
  - Simply click the Share icon in the toolbar and select **Go to Channel to go straight to the story's channel.**

You have the option to disable the Today feed's suggestions for specific channels and subjects, like food or travel. Click the **More button** next to the item in the feed, and select Stop Suggesting. Go for it and follow it if you decide to change your mind and want Apple News to recommend the channel or subject again.

Track stocks and the market

You can personalize your watchlists to show the ticker icons you frequently check. A ticker symbol is added to both the My Symbols watchlist and the watchlist you establish. Your whole collection of ticker symbols is included in the My Symbols watchlist; the watchlists you make only include the ticker icons you add to them. To include a ticker symbol in your list, you do not need to be familiar with it. It's sufficient to know the name to get going.

Find and add new ticker icons

Look up the ticker symbols you wish to keep an eye on and include them in your watch lists.

- Click the name of the watchlist that is now active at the top of the sidebar in the **Stocks app on your Mac, and then select a watchlist.**
- Use the search box to enter a name or ticker symbol.
- Take one of the subsequent actions:
  - To add the ticker symbol to both the current watchlist and the My Symbols watchlist, click the Add button located next to it in the sidebar.
  - To add the ticker symbol to the current watchlist, the My Symbols watchlist, and any other watchlists you want, click **the symbol in the sidebar and then click the Add to Watchlist button in the toolbar.**

Select the **Delete button** in the search field to empty it and go back to your watchlist. The currency code and the exchange on which the ticker symbol is traded are displayed for each entry in the list of search results. Use the fact that many stocks trade on many exchanges to your advantage when selecting which ticker sign to add to your watchlists.

CHAPTER 14

SUBSCRIBE TO SERVICES

Apple Music

You may listen to millions of songs from the Apple Music catalog in addition to your music library with Apple Music, an ad-free streaming music subscription. You may make your playlists, stream, and download lossless and Dolby Atmos audio files receive tailored recommendations, discover what music your friends are enjoying, view special video content, and much more as a subscriber. You can listen whenever you want, online or off. You have the option to sign up for Apple One, which comes with Apple Music and other Apple services, or for Apple Music alone.

Subscribe to Apple Music

- Go to **Account > Join Apple Music in the Mac's Music app.**
- Observe the directions displayed on the screen. You might be prompted to use your Apple ID to log in. You can create an Apple ID during setup if you don't already have one.

Cancel or alter your Apple Music subscription

- Select **Account > Account Settings** from within the Mac Music app, and then log in.
- You might be prompted to use your Apple ID to log in.
- Choose **Manage next to Subscriptions in the Settings section**.
- Choose between the following actions after selecting **Edit next to Apple Music or Apple One:**
  - **Cancel:** Select Cancel Subscription and adhere to the prompts displayed on the screen.
  - **Modify:** Select a different plan or click Select Individual Services, then adhere to the prompts on the screen.

Apple TV+

Channels that are accessible through the Apple TV app, such as MLS Season Pass and Apple TV+, are available for subscription. With new content introduced every month, Apple TV+ is a subscription streaming service that offers a variety of Apple Originals, including comedy, kids' entertainment, dramas, captivating dramas, and pioneering documentaries. Watch all live Major League Soccer regular-season matches, the whole playoff run, and the

Leagues Cup without any blackouts when you subscribe to MLS Season Pass. To watch the shows you desire, subscribe to Apple TV channels like Starz, Paramount+, and others.

Subscribe to Apple TV+

- On your Mac, open **the Apple TV app.**
- In the sidebar, select **Apple TV+.**
- After selecting the subscription option, adhere to the on-screen directions. To begin your free trial, **sign in if you already have an Apple ID.**

Note: By purchasing Apple One, you have the option to combine your Apple TV+ membership with other Apple services.

Subscribe to Apple TV channels

- On your Mac, open **the Apple TV app.**
- Within the sidebar, select **Store.**
- To view Apple TV channels, scroll down to Add Channels, then move the cursor to the right and choose an item.
- After selecting the subscription option, adhere to the on-screen directions.

The Channels header rises to the top of any subscribed channels in the sidebar when you become an Apple TV channel subscriber. You can access a channel's main page directly by clicking on it in the sidebar.

Cancel a subscription

- On your Mac, select **Account > Account Settings from within the Apple TV app. You might be prompted to use your Apple ID to log in.**
- Navigate to the Settings area by scrolling down the Account Information box.
- To modify or cancel a subscription, choose Manage next to Subscriptions, select **Edit next to a subscription, and then follow the on-screen directions.**
- When you're done, click **Done after swiping down, and then click Done again in the Account Information window.**

Apple Arcade

You may download and play a variety of innovative new games from the App Store—on all of your compatible devices—if you have an Apple Arcade subscription. Apple Arcade and Apple One, which combines Apple Arcade with other services, are both available for subscription.

Note: Not all nations or areas have access to Apple Arcade or Apple One. Check out the Apple Support article on Apple Media Services' Availability. The compatibility of hardware and software determines whether Apple Arcade games are available on which devices. Not all places may have access to all content.

Subscribe to Apple Arcade

- On your Mac, select **Arcade from the sidebar of the App Store.**
- After selecting the subscription option, adhere to the on-screen directions.

Cancel or alter your Apple Arcade subscription

- Hit your name in the lower-left corner of the Mac App Store, or choose Sign In if you haven't already.
- Go to **Account Settings and click.**
- To edit Apple Arcade or Apple One subscriptions, select **Manage next to Subscriptions in the Manage section.**
- Observe the directions displayed on the screen. As long as it's at least one day before the subscription expires, you can cancel it whenever you like.

You can utilize Family Sharing to share Apple Arcade with up to five more family members if you have an Apple Arcade or Apple One subscription. There is nothing you need to do for the members of your family group; Apple Arcade will be available to them as soon as your membership starts. If you are a current member of a Family Sharing group that has a membership to Apple Arcade or Apple One, you utilize the group's subscription rather than having your own renewed on your subsequent billing date. Your subscription is used by the family group you join if it doesn't have a subscription.

Apple News+

With Apple News+, you can access information from premium digital publishers, popular newspapers, and hundreds of publications from within Apple News on your Mac. Apple News+ and other Apple services are included in Apple One Premier, which is also available for subscription.

Subscribe to Apple News+

- Choose News+ in the sidebar of the Mac News app (click the **Sidebar icon** in the toolbar if the sidebar isn't visible), and then hit **the subscription button.**
- Observe the directions displayed on the screen. The App Store may ask you to log in with your Apple ID.

Cancel or change your Apple News+ subscription

- On your Mac, select **File > Manage Subscriptions** from within the News app. The App Store may ask you to log in with your Apple ID.
- Select Manage next to Subscriptions in the Manage area, and then select **Apple News+ or Apple One to edit.**
- Observe the directions displayed on the screen.

You can utilize Family Sharing to share Apple News+ with up to five more family members if you have an Apple News+ or Apple One Premier subscription. Members of your family group don't need to take any action; as soon as they launch the News app after your membership starts, they will have access to Apple News+. If you already have a subscription to Apple News+ or Apple One Premier and you join a Family Sharing group that has one, you use the group's subscription rather than having your own renewed on your next billing date. Your subscription is used by the family group you join if it doesn't have a subscription.

Podcasts shows and channels

A channel is an assortment of programs that a podcast producer offers. In addition to subscribing to other services for early or exclusive access to subscriber-only audio, ad-free listening, and other benefits, you can listen to free shows and channels.

Note: Not all nations or areas offer subscription services.

- Choose **the show or channel you wish to subscribe to in the Mac's Podcasts app.** You automatically follow a show when you subscribe to it.
- Press **the button to subscribe.** Podcasts indicate that you already have access if someone in your family group subscribes to a show or channel when you're utilizing Family Sharing. You might be prompted to provide your password and Apple ID. Make sure the Apple ID you use to log in is the same one you use to make purchases from iTunes and App Stores.
- Select a subscription plan (annual or monthly, for example) that the podcast maker offers. By selecting Channels in the sidebar, you can easily access a channel that you have subscribed to.

Connect app subscriptions to Podcasts

If you enrolled through the App Store and the app supports audio material in Podcasts, your eligible app subscriptions are instantly linked to Podcasts.

If you made your subscription differently, take these actions:

- On your Mac, launch the Podcasts app, then go through or search for a channel that you can subscribe to.

202

- To connect your app subscription, click the **Already a Subscriber link on the Channel page and follow the prompts.**

View Apple family subscriptions

You can share your Mac subscriptions with family members for Apple Music, Apple TV+, Apple Arcade, Apple News+, and other services. To view the services you can share with family members, use the Family Sharing Subscriptions options.

- Select **Apple menu > System Settings, select Family** in the sidebar, choose **Subscriptions on the right, and finally select Apple Subscriptions to see the available subscriptions.**

Set up Family Sharing if you do not see it in the sidebar.

Apple Subscriptions for your family: To learn more about a service or to manage your current subscriptions, select the **Learn More icon next to it.**

It is possible to share your Apple service subscriptions with family members. You can share over 90 million songs with your Family Sharing group, for instance, by setting up an Apple Music Family Plan membership. When new services are launched, the list's subscriptions are updated accordingly.

CHAPTER 15

PRIVACY, SECURITY, AND ACCESSIBILITY

Guard your privacy

When utilizing applications that share data online, privacy is a major concern. Security measures in macOS are designed to protect your privacy and limit the amount of information that is publicly available online about you and your Mac.

Use Screen Time

Screen Time is a useful tool for keeping an eye on your kids' computer usage and limiting their internet access.

- Select System Settings from the Apple menu, and then select Screen Time from the sidebar. (You might have to scroll below.)

Use the privacy features in Safari

There are a lot of features in Safari that let you manage your online privacy. Safari doesn't save a record of the websites you visit or the things you download because you have the option to browse secretly. To find out who was prevented from following you, you can view your privacy report. On your Mac, you can delete cookies, permit or prohibit pop-up windows, and more.

Control the personal information you share with apps

Web browsers and other programs can receive and use location-based data thanks to location services. You have the option to fully disable Location Services or limit which apps can access your location data. Certain apps can collect and utilize data from your calendar, contacts, images, and reminders. Certain apps might be able to use your Mac's camera or microphone.

Choose whether to share analytics information

You have the power to assist Apple in raising the caliber and functionality of its goods and services. Your Mac's analytics data can be automatically gathered by macOS and sent to Apple for review. The data is provided to Apple anonymously and is only shared with your permission. Utilize the Privacy & Security options to select whether analytics data is forwarded to Apple.

Select System Settings from the Apple menu, and then click Privacy & Security in the sidebar. Next, select Analytics & Improvements from the list on the right.

Set up a firewall

A firewall can help you keep your privacy safe by preventing unauthorized network communications from happening on your Mac. You can also utilize "stealth mode," which stops other people from finding your Mac online if the firewall is activated. Network settings can be used to configure and personalize your firewall.

- Select System Settings from the Apple menu, and then select Network in the sidebar and Firewall on the right.

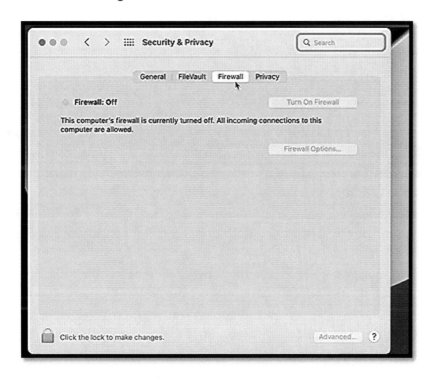

Use Mail Privacy Protection

You can safeguard your privacy with the Mail app. Email communications you receive might contain remote content, which enables the sender to gather data when you see the message, including your IP address, when and how often you view it, and whether you transmit it. Senders are prevented from learning your information by Mail Privacy Protection. You can enable Protect Mail Activity in Mail settings if you didn't when you initially opened Mail with macOS Ventura.

- Click **Privacy after selecting Mail > Settings** in the Mac Mail program. Click on **Safeguard Mail Activity**. If you choose this option, when you get a message (rather than when you see it), remote content is downloaded discreetly in the background and your IP address is hidden from senders.

You have the option to block all remote content and hide your IP address separately if you deselect this option. If you opt to Block All Remote Content, when you view the message, a banner indicating that it contains remote content appears; you can then choose to download the content.

Note: When utilizing a Wi-Fi or Ethernet network, your IP address remains visible to senders even if you disabled the option in the network settings to restrict IP address tracking.

Control access to your camera

You can take pictures and videos with your Mac's camera by installing certain programs. Which apps are permitted to use the camera is up to you.

- Select **System Settings from the Apple menu, then select Privacy & Security from the** sidebar.
- On the right, select **Camera**. Update to macOS Mojave or later if you are unable to see the Camera.
- For every app on the list, toggle camera access on or off. The list displays installed apps that have requested access to your camera.

You haven't installed any camera-using apps if there are none on the list. Apps that come with your Mac, such as FaceTime and Photo Booth, have automatic access; you don't have to provide it to them.

Note: When you launch a camera-capable app, the camera automatically turns on. The presence of a green light beside the camera signifies that it is turned on. When you exit or close every app that uses the camera, the camera (as well as the green light) goes out.

To grant a website permission to use the camera in Safari, go to **Safari > Settings, choose Websites, and then click Camera.**

Use Sign in with Apple for apps and websites

Using Apple Sign-in to access apps and websites is a simple and private method. It makes it easier to sign in every time by using your Apple ID to safely create an account with an app or website. You don't need to fill out a form, validate your email address, or pick a new password.

Create an account for an app or website

- When an app or website on your Mac asks you to register, click the icon to sign in or, if it's not accessible, to proceed with Apple.
- Keep the following in mind while you follow the on-screen instructions:
  - Click **the Name field and type a different name** if you would rather not use your real name.
  - Select the email address to use for the app or website if you have several email addresses linked to your Apple ID in the Apple ID settings.
  - Click **Hide My Email** if you would rather keep your email address hidden. Emails from the app or website are forwarded to your actual email address using a randomly generated email address by Apple.

Sign in to your account for an app or website

- Select the button to log in or proceed with Apple on your Mac.
- If your Mac or Magic Keyboard supports Touch ID, use it. If not, enter your login password on your Mac (you might also need to enter your Apple ID password).

Using the same Apple ID, you may sign in from your other devices as well, including your iPhone, iPad, Apple Watch, and Apple TV.

Set up your Mac to be secure

Here are some steps you may take to increase the security of your Mac.

Use secure passwords

You should use passwords to safeguard your Mac and pick difficult-to-guess passwords to protect your data.

Create passkeys

Using a passkey eliminates the need to generate and remember a password to access an app or website account. A passkey employs Touch ID or Face ID to verify your identity instead of a password.

Require users to log in

You should create distinct users for each person using the Mac and make sure they all log in if someone else has physical access to the machine. This stops someone who isn't authorized from using the Mac. Users can only access their files and settings because it also divides user files. Other users' files and settings are not visible to or editable by other users.

Secure your Mac when it's idle

If your Mac hasn't been used for a while, you can configure it to log out the current user. View when not in use; configure your Mac to log out. It should also demand a password to exit the screen saver or rouse it from sleep. You can program a hot corner to be clicked whenever you want to quickly lock your screen for convenience.

Limit the number of administrative users

On a Mac, administrator rights can be shared by one or more persons. The administrator is automatically the one who set up the Mac in the first place. Administrators can install and remove software, modify settings, and add, manage, and remove other users. When administrator capabilities are not required, an administrator should create a regular user account. The potential impact is significantly less if an ordinary user's security is breached than if the user has administrator capabilities. If your Mac is shared by several people, restrict the amount of users who have administrator access.

Keep your data safe

Make frequent backups, restrict who can access your data, install software updates, take steps to locate or disable a lost machine, and stay away from malware to safeguard the data on your Mac.

Perform regular backups

Always make a backup of your Mac. You can then quickly retrieve your files if something goes wrong with your Mac or if you inadvertently erase something. Setting up a Time Machine, which automatically backs up all of the data on your Mac every day, is the simplest way to create backups. You have a few more options for backing up your crucial files besides Time Machine, such as creating CDs and DVDs and moving files to an external drive.

Limited unwanted access to your information

Many features in macOS are designed to help protect the data on your Mac. You should create separate user accounts for each person using your Mac if you have numerous users so that no one can alter the files that another needs. Ensure that all user accounts have passwords, use strong passwords to prevent illegal access, and disable automatic login in the Users & Groups settings.

- Select **Apple menu > System options**, and then tap **Users & Groups** in the sidebar to access the Users & Groups options.

Install software updates promptly

By default, your Mac is configured to search automatically for software updates and to notify you when new versions are ready for download. Download and install these updates—which include the most recent security software—as soon as they become available to prevent viruses and other problems.

- Select **System Settings from the Apple menu**, and then click **General in the sidebar**. Next, select Software Update from the list of available updates on the right.

If you try to check for updates and nothing happens, you might be offline.

Create a passkey

Using a passkey eliminates the need to generate and remember a password to access an app or website account. A passkey employs Touch ID or Face ID to verify your identity instead of a password. You can use Touch ID to log in if your Mac or Magic Keyboard has it. Moreover, you may use Face ID to authenticate yourself when logging in with an iPhone or iPad by scanning a QR code.

Create a passkey for a new account

Enter the account name when creating a new account, then click "Submit."
- You need to set up iCloud Keychain on your Mac before you can create a passkey.
- Select your preferred method of login when you see the option to save a passkey for the account:
  - Put your finger on the Touch ID sensor on your Mac to use Touch ID.
  - Using your iPhone or iPad, scan a QR code: Select Other Options.
  - Key for external security: Select Other.

Sign in to an account with a passkey

- Enter your account name in the designated field on the account sign-in screen, and then click it.
- In the list of suggestions, click your account.
- **Take one of the subsequent actions:**

- Touch the Touch ID sensor with your finger if your Mac has this feature.
- If you possess an iPad or iPhone: After selecting "Passkey from nearby device" under Other Options, click the QR code.
- **Note:** On your iPhone or iPad, go to **Settings > Bluetooth and turn on Bluetooth®. Your Mac must also have Bluetooth enabled.**
- External security key: Select "Security key" from the Other Options menu, then adhere to the on-screen directions.

Understand passwords

MacOS is built to protect and safeguard your data. Using strong passwords in critical areas is crucial to your Mac's security.

Login Password

You need a login password, sometimes known as a user password, to access the data on your Mac. Make sure your login password is simple to remember, write it down, and save it somewhere safe when you create it.

Apple ID password

You can use an Apple ID to access FaceTime, iCloud, Apple Books, the iTunes Store, the App Store, and other Apple services. It consists of a password and an email address (daniel_rico1@icloud.com, for instance). Utilizing a single Apple ID across all Apple services is advised by Apple. Make sure your Apple ID password is simple to remember, write it down, and store it somewhere safe when you create it.

Website passwords

When creating a password for a website, Safari recommends using a distinct, difficult-to-guess password, also known as a "strong" password. Using the given password or making your passkey is advised. When you need to log in again, your keychain will automatically fill in your saved passwords and passkeys.

Use the Passwords settings to view or modify the passwords and passkeys you have saved for websites.
- Select **System Settings** from the Apple menu, then select **Passwords** from the sidebar.

Passwords keychains

Your passwords are automatically entered when you sign in to websites, apps, and services thanks to a keychain that stores them. **Passwords can be kept in both iCloud Keychain and Keychain Access.**

- **Keychain Access**: This Mac tool keeps passwords for several different services and applications. The password that you use to unlock your keychain is the same as the one you use to get into your Mac.
- **iCloud Keychain**: Across your Mac, iPhone, iPad, and iPod touch, iCloud Keychain maintains your passwords current. Passwords for websites and Wi-Fi networks are stored, and account passwords and configurations added to your Mac's Internet Account settings are maintained.

About your recovery key

You have two options if you use FileVault to secure the data on your Mac: utilizing a recovery key or your iCloud account to unlock your disk and reset your login password if you forget it. An alphanumeric string that is generated specifically for you is known as a recovery key. The recovery key should not be kept in the same place as the Mac, as this is where it can be found.

Keep your Apple ID secure

You may access Apple services like the App Store, Apple Music, iCloud, iMessage, FaceTime, and more using your Apple ID. Your account contains the contact, payment, and security information you use for all Apple services, in addition to the email address and password you use to log in.

Below are best practices for maximizing the security of your Apple ID;

- Never give up your Apple ID to anybody, not even close relatives. If you ever lose access to your account, you can designate up to five reliable individuals as Account Recovery Contacts. Additionally, you can designate someone as a Legacy Contact if you pass away.
- Never provide anybody else access to your password, security questions, verification codes, recovery key, or any other account-related information. Apple will never request this information from you.
- Never use the password for your Apple ID to access other online accounts.
- It is important to always sign out of a public computer after you are done using it to keep other people from accessing your account.
- Give your account protection using two-factor authentication. When you create a new Apple ID on a device running macOS 10.15.4, iOS 13.4, iPadOS 13.4, or later, two-factor authentication is automatically enabled for your account. It is recommended that you enable two-factor authentication if you previously established an Apple ID account without it.

Get started with accessibility features

Numerous accessibility tools in macOS are available to help your needs in speech, hearing, movement, and vision. If you need them sometimes or continuously, these features make using your Mac easier. When configuring your Mac, or at any time later, you can enter the accessibility settings to enable accessibility features. Select System Preferences from the Apple menu on your Mac, and then select Accessibility from the sidebar.

Vision

Features for accessibility in macOS make it simpler to view what's on the screen. Additionally, you can speak what's on the screen with your Mac. To pronounce the text in Windows, documents, and webpages as well as what's on the screen, use VoiceOver, the Mac's built-in screen reader. With VoiceOver, you can use trackpad motions, a refreshable braille display, or the keyboard to operate your Mac. Use VoiceOver Utility to personalize VoiceOver.

Zoom features

- Zoom in on a portion of the screen or the full thing to make the content on it larger and easier to see. You have the option to independently adjust the zoom on any additional displays you use.
- To view a larger version of whatever is beneath the pointer—such as text you are typing or reading, or text and icons in the user interface—use Hover Text.
- To view a larger version of the Touch Bar on your Mac, enable Touch Bar zoom if any of the elements in the Touch Bar are difficult to see.

Display features

- To change the text reading size for a variety of apps and system functions, use a single slider.
- Change the pointer's color, size, or size as you move it quickly to make it easier to see on the screen.
- Adding a color filter or tint, lowering transparency, or inverting colors can all help to make the content on the screen easier to see and distinguish.
- When you view media that shows flashing or strobing lights, when you start apps or go-between desktops, or when you view quickly animated visuals (like GIFs), the screen may stop or become less motion.

Note: "Dim flashing lights" are limited to Mac machines equipped with Apple silicon and compatible media. It is not appropriate to use it to treat any medical ailment. Real-time content processing occurs on the device.

Hearing

Real-time text (RTT) calls, the ability to configure and display captions on the screen, and many other accessibility features are built into macOS.

Hearing devices features

Connect your Mac to Made for iPhone hearing aids, and then tweak their settings. Note: Only some Mac computers with the M1 chip and all Mac computers with the M2 or M3 chip can be paired with Made for iPhone hearing aids.

Audio features

You can play stereo music as mono and set the screen to flash when notifications or announcements are made. In addition, you can play background sounds and adjust accessibility settings for Apple earbuds and earphones that are associated with your Mac. You can select whether Spatial Audio tracks your head movements when you listen to Spatial Audio content if your Mac is equipped with Apple hardware.

Live captions features

With the use of on-device intelligence, your Mac can caption audio in real time, making it easier for you to follow along with audio and video chats. It should be noted that Live Captions (beta) is limited to Mac machines equipped with Apple hardware and isn't accessible in all languages, nations, or areas. Live captions' accuracy can vary, so in critical or high-risk scenarios, you shouldn't rely on them.

Mobility

With the help of accessibility capabilities in macOS, you can use an onscreen keyboard, assistive devices, spoken instructions, and other alternate ways to manipulate the cursor to navigate and interact with your Mac. Moreover, you may configure the interface to make using a mouse or trackpad easier.

Voice Control features

- You can interact with the screen; navigate the desktop and programs, dictate and edit text, and more by speaking commands with Voice Control.
- You can label on-screen items or display a numbered grid to make it simpler to pick items and navigate the screen if the name of an item on the screen isn't obvious or if you need to interact with a specific area of the screen.
- Though you can use a custom vocabulary and construct your instructions, macOS comes with a standard set of Voice Control commands.

Keyboard features

- You can use the Tab key and other keys to traverse all UI elements on your Mac without a mouse or trackpad when you enable Full Keyboard Access.
- On a physical keyboard, Slow Keys and Sticky Keys facilitate key pressing.
- You can use your Mac without a physical keyboard by turning on the Accessibility Keyboard, which activates an onscreen keyboard. It offers customizable navigation options and sophisticated typing (such as typing suggestions) for using your preferred apps.
- You can use the Accessibility Keyboard to activate Dwell, which uses eye- or head-tracking technology to perform mouse actions.

Pointer Control features

- Configure the mouse and trackpad's user interface. For instance, change how quickly the mouse or trackpad responds when you double-click an object. Alternatively, you can drag objects using three fingers, drag lock, or neither. With alternate pointer actions, you can utilize keyboard keys, assistive switches, or facial expressions (such as a smile or an open mouth) to carry out mouse movements (like a left-click or drag-and-drop action).
- Using Mouse Keys, you can use a numeric keypad or a keyboard to move the pointer and hit the **mouse button.**
- When you use a head pointer, the Mac's built-in or attached camera will move the pointer in response to movements of your face or head.

Switch Control

With Switch Control, you may operate your Mac and input text while interacting with objects on the screen and using one or more adaptive devices. Until you choose an item or use a switch to execute an action, Switch Control searches a panel or the user interface.

Speech

You may get your typing to be read out, have a synthetic voice that sounds like you, and more with the accessibility tools included in macOS.

Live Speech

Synthesized speech can be used to have what you type spoken aloud in in-person discussions or through apps such as FaceTime if you are mute or have lost your ability to speak over time.

Personal Voice

It is possible to produce an artificial voice that sounds just like you if you are in danger of losing your capacity to speak.

Note: Not all languages are supported by Personal Voice, and it is only available on Mac computers equipped with Apple silicon. Only Live Speech and third-party apps that you authorize, including AAC (Augmentative and Alternative Communication) apps, can be utilized with Personal Voice. Personal Voice may only be used to record a voice that closely resembles your voice on a device for private, non-commercial purposes.

CHAPTER 16

ACCESSORIES AND HARDWARE

Connect an external display

Your Mac's capabilities may allow you to connect more than one display. This can be something you wish to do to free up more screen space, or to make it easier to work in various apps and switch between them.

Identify the video ports on your Mac

Before connecting displays, you must ascertain the kind of video ports on your Mac. What kind and number of external displays you can connect, as well as how are determined by the ports you have.

See the number of displays your Mac supports

The next step is to find out how many displays you wish to connect to your Mac.
- Thunderbolt 3 (USB-C): One monitor can be connected to each Thunderbolt 3 (USB-C) connector on Mac laptops. The Thunderbolt 3 display needs to be the last device in the chain if you connect several Thunderbolt devices. You can use the USB ports on your Thunderbolt 3 display for power and data.
- Mini DisplayPort: Up to two screens can be connected to Mac computers equipped with Mini DisplayPort. In a chain of connected Thunderbolt devices, a DisplayPort device needs to be the last device.
- For Mac computers with Thunderbolt or Thunderbolt 2, you can connect up to two screens. If the displays have Thunderbolt connectors, you can connect one to another before connecting one to your Mac's Thunderbolt port. If your Mac has two Thunderbolt connections, you can connect each monitor separately.
- For Macs equipped with Thunderbolt 4 (USB-C) and HDMI ports: You can attach up to eight external monitors to your Mac, depending on the model.

Ensure you have the right cables and adapters

- If your displays include cables that match the ports on your Mac, you can use these to connect the display to your Mac.
- If your displays do not have cables, get ones that fit into the accessible ports on your Mac and monitors.

- If your display connections' connectors do not match the ports on your Mac, you may be allowed to use an adapter.

Connect your displays to your Mac

Connect your displays to your Mac using the correct video ports, cables, and adapters (if necessary). Once your displays are linked, you may want to change their settings. To view your display's settings,

- Go to **the Apple menu and select System Settings, then Displays in the sidebar.** You also have the option of extending or mirroring your Mac desktop across numerous external screens.

If you have a third-party display, consult the paperwork that came with it for further information on the monitor's video ports and connections, as well as to ensure that you are connecting the display following the manufacturer's specifications.

Use the built-in camera

Many Mac computers include a built-in FaceTime or FaceTime HD camera near the top border of the display. When you start an app (such as FaceTime or Photo Booth) or use a camera-capable feature (such as Markup or head pointer), the camera turns on automatically. A green light beside the camera illuminates to show that the camera is turned on. When you close or exit all apps or functions that can use the camera, the camera (along with the green light) turns off.

Do the following to improve the quality of the image;

- Clean the camera with a soft, lint-free cloth.
- Adjust the lighting: Make sure you're well-lit from the front, with no bright spots behind you, such as windows in front of you.
- Improve your Wi-Fi connection by moving closer to your router and ensuring that no objects, such as walls, are hindering the signal.
- Change app settings: Some apps may allow you to customize camera quality. Check your app's settings and change as needed.
- Link to a supported iPhone and utilize its camera rather than the Mac's built-in camera.

Connect a Bluetooth device

Link your Mac to a Bluetooth® keyboard, mouse, trackpad, headset, or other audio device.

Connect a Bluetooth device

- Ensure that the device is switched on and discoverable (further information can be found in the device's documentation).
- On your Mac, select **Apple menu** > **System Settings**, then **Bluetooth** from the sidebar. You may need to scroll down.

- Keep the pointer over the device in the list and then select **Connect**. If prompted, click **Accept (or type a series of numbers and hit Enter).**

A Bluetooth device can also be connected to your Mac by selecting it from the menu bar's Bluetooth status symbol. If the icon does not appear in the menu bar, you can add it utilizing Control Center settings.

Use AirPods with your Mac

When your AirPods are nearby and ready to pair with your Mac, you may use them to listen to music, use Siri, or make phone calls.

Pair your AirPods with your Mac

- Open the lid on your AirPods case.

- Hold down either the setup icon on the back of the case or the noise control button (AirPods Max only) until the status light flashes white.
- On your Mac, navigate to the **Apple menu > System Settings, then Bluetooth in the** sidebar.
- Hold the pointer over your AirPods in the device list on the right, then select **Connect.** You can configure your AirPods to connect automatically or just when they were last linked to your Mac.

Optimize your Mac battery life

Your Mac is built to be energy efficient right out of the box, with features like Compressed Memory and App Nap that help you stay fast while saving power. However, there are various strategies to improve energy efficiency. Some of the settings may be unavailable based on your Mac.

Put your Mac to sleep

Your Mac remains turned on while sleeping, but it consumes far less energy. Awakening your Mac from sleep requires less time than booting it up.
- On your Mac, select **Apple menu > Sleep.**

Get the most from your battery

If you have a Mac laptop, you can adjust the settings below to save energy and extend the life of your battery.
- On your Mac, select **Apple menu -> System Settings,** then **Battery in the sidebar.** You'll probably need to scroll down.
- Do one of the following:
  - Choose the **pop-up menu beside Low Power Mode** on the right, and then select **Always, Only on Battery, or Only on Power Adapter.**

  - Click the **Info button next to Battery Health on the right,** then select Optimized Battery Charging and "Manage battery longevity."

- ○ Click **Options** on the right, then enable "Put hard disks to sleep when possible" and "Automatic graphics switching."

Dim the display

Reduce the display brightness to the lowest comfortable level. For example, in a dark environment, the display may be dimmer than in bright sunshine. To dim the display, use your keyboard's brightness keys or the Displays settings. If you're using a Mac laptop, you can also configure your display to dim automatically when you're on battery power.

Turn off Wi-Fi and Bluetooth

If you don't require Bluetooth® or Wi-Fi, turn them off. They use energy even when they are not in use.

- To disable Bluetooth on your Mac, go to the Apple menu and select System Settings, then Bluetooth in the sidebar. You may need to scroll down. Turn off Bluetooth on the right.
- To turn off Wi-Fi on your Mac, go to the Apple menu and select **System Settings**, then Network in the sidebar. You may need to scroll down. Select Wi-Fi from the list on the right, and then turn it off.

Optimize storage space

macOS can help you free up space on your Mac by optimizing its storage. For example, when space is limited, you can save files, images and videos, Apple TV movies and shows, and email attachments in iCloud, where they are accessible on demand. Files do not take up space on your Mac, and you may download the original files whenever you need them. Recent files and optimized versions of your images are always available on your Mac.

- On your Mac, select **Apple menu -> System Settings**, then General in the sidebar. You may need to scroll down.
- Click the **Storage button on the right.**
- View the recommendations and determine how to improve your Mac's storage.

Burn CDs and DVDs

If your Mac has an external DVD drive (such as an Apple USB SuperDrive), you can permanently save or burn files to CDs and DVDs for file sharing, file transfer, or backup purposes. Discs burned on your Mac can be used on Windows and other machines.

- Put a blank disc into the optical drive. If a dialog box displays, click **the pop-up menu and select Open Finder**. If you want the Finder to open whenever you insert a blank disc, select **"Make this action the default". The DVD will appear on your desktop.**
- Double-click the disc to open the dialog, and then drag the files and folders you would like to burn on it. Aliases for the files are placed in the disc's window. The initial files are not transferred or erased. **Note:** If you are interested in burning the same files to disks several times, use a burn folder.
- Organize and rename the files. Whenever the disc is burned, the things on it retain the same names and places as they do in the disc window. After the CD has been burned, you cannot edit the items.
- Select **File > Burn [disk]** and then follow the on-screen directions. The files that the aliases refer to are burned to the CD. Furthermore, if the folders you add to the disk contain aliases, the files they refer to are likewise burned on the DVD. If you remove the disc without burning it, a burn folder containing the items copied to the disc is produced and saved to your desktop. To finish the burn process later, click the Burn icon next to the folder in the Finder sidebar, or hold down the Control key while clicking **any disk and selecting Burn disk from the shortcut menu.**

To burn a disc image (.dmg file) to a disk, Control-click it, select "**Burn Disc Image [disc name] to Disc " from the shortcut menu,** and follow the instructions. To wipe the data of a rewritable disc, Control-click the optical drive in the Finder's sidebar and select wipe Rewritable Disc from the shortcut menu.

Control accessories in your home

Items you add to Home are organized into five categories at the top of the Home screen:
- Climate
- Lights
- Security
- Speakers and TVs
- Water

Accessories are listed separately in other parts, such as the rooms you've added, in addition to the categories. Tap **Discover** in the sidebar to learn more about utilizing suitable accessories for smart homes with the Home app.

Control an accessory

To turn an item on or off, use the Home app on your Mac and click **its icon on the tile.** To access the available controls, click **the accessory's name in the tile.** The available controls vary depending on the type of accessory. For example, certain light bulbs allow you to modify the brightness or color. Set-top boxes and streaming sticks may just include an **Activate button.**

Control an accessory with various features

A single accessory tile controls numerous functionalities. For example, if you have a ceiling fan with a built-in light, you may regulate the fan's speed and the light's brightness using the same tile. The sensors are organized by accessory category at the top of the screen. **The available controls vary depending on the type of accessory.**
- On your Mac, open **the Home app and select the tile of an accessory with numerous functionalities.**
- Click **on a feature to control or view it.**

Move an accessory to another room

- You can either add or move an accessory from one area to another.
- On your Mac, open the Home app and select Home or a room from the sidebar.
- Drag the accessory tile into a room from the sidebar.

Conclusion

The MacBook Air M3 exemplifies Apple's constant innovation and commitment to providing high-performance, user-friendly gadgets. With its powerful M3 chip, the MacBook Air pushes the limits of what an ultra-portable notebook can do, providing an unrivaled combination of speed, efficiency, and versatility. The arrival of the M3 chip represents a huge leap in processing power and energy economy, transforming the MacBook Air into not only a powerful performer for demanding work but also a dependable companion for everyday use. The perfect integration of hardware and software improves the user experience, allowing professionals, students, and creative to easily handle a wide range of tasks, from demanding graphic design to complex data processing and casual surfing. The MacBook Air's elegant and lightweight form, combined with its bright Retina display and exceptional battery life, allows users to work, create, and enjoy themselves with unparalleled portability and flair. Furthermore, the addition of advanced features such as expanded connectivity choices, greater thermal management, and superior audio quality solidifies its position as a flexible tool in today's digital landscape. In conclusion, the MacBook Air M3 is more than just a laptop; it ushers in a new era of computing. It represents the ultimate blend of style and function, making it an excellent choice for anyone looking for a powerful, dependable, and visually appealing smartphone. Whether for professional, academic, or personal use, the MacBook Air M3 redefines what a modern laptop can and ought to be.

INDEX

D

E

F

G

P

V

W

Y

Made in the USA
Middletown, DE
30 August 2024

59979366R00144